The Ministry
of a
Deacon

Ronnie Aitchison

DEDICATION

This book owes much to many people, to John Vincent, who started me on the path; to my tutors Michael Jarrat and Eric Wright, without whose patience and generosity it would not have happened; to my friend and UTU colleague, Stephen Smyth who not only picked me up when I stumbled, but sometimes carried me; and to my wife Pat, who has read all of it too many times. To these and others I owe a debt of gratitude.

CONTENTS

INTRODUCTION TO THIS EDITION

The Ministry of A Deacon has been out of print for some years but there has been some interest in acquiring copies from those interested in the Methodist Diaconal Order and so I have decided to produce a reprint. While I am confident that Part One and Part Three are as relevant today as they were when the book was first printed There has been no attempt to update the information regarding the role of the diaconate in other denominations found in Part Two. Some of the denominational situations have developed in the interim, but my comments were accurate for the time of my original research.

The situation in Methodism has continued to develop. There were some significant changes as the book was being prepared for publication and I will address these later in this section. As can be seen in the original text, Methodist thinking and attitudes to the Order have been in continual flux. The theology is still a matter being investigated.

Some differences which have taken place since the time of the project (1996-2000) include the most significant, the change in standing of the deacons which led to a momentous moment in Conference in 1998 when the deacons to be ordained were for the first time Received Into Full Connexion. At this point in the proceedings, the president invited all deacons (and deaconesses) present to stand and included them in the reception. I was present in the gallery and was able to observe that it was crowded with members of the Order retired and active and the sense of confirmation was tangible. What this meant was that deacons were now included as ministers of and part of the ministry of the church. This followed a long period of discussion at Faith and Order and the other committees of the church. The change had been resisted at first as there was a residual understanding that Methodism had only one ordained ministry, the acceptance that there are two such orders in our church has forced the change of terminology in standing orders that was most hard fought, the use of presbyter as a differentiation in the general term for minister. Closely following this step, the situation regarding dispensation to preside at communion became a matter of greater concern. This had always been a sensitive matter, but gradually the stance of the church and the Order became more firm and the position now seems to be that a dispensation for a deacon should not be granted other than in exceptional circumstances. The position of deacons in regard to the leadership of the church was a difficult one to resolve. Some had suggested that there should be no barrier to deacons becoming President of Conference, but this was always a questionable stance with regard to many of the duties of the President, and possibly a sense that this would create confusion about authority. That the office of Vice-President had been held by deacons up to that time forced the only pragmatic decision which was to make that office open to lay people and deacons.

Stationing for deacons is still operated within the understanding of "a sending". They do not negotiate with circuits as the appointments are arranged through the Diaconal Stationing Sub-committee. But, in line with the change in status brought in in 1998 district and connexional stationing committees have a much greater involvement.

For many years the matter of the wearing of a "dog collar" by a deacon has been debated at Convocation. For much of this time, the feeling at Convocation was opposed to this. At the point when I entered the Order in 1993 the uniform for a deacon was described as blazer or suit, a white shirt and, for men a diaconal tie, the badge of the Order was worn by all. This had been important to the Wesley Deaconesses but gradually there was slippage. Polo shirts and sweatshirts with the badge embroidered on became common and gradually uniform lost its significance. In the polo shirt I was mistaken for an ambulance man at a hospital. Recent statements regarding uniform suggest that there is no required uniform for the deacons. During my active service I was to become very aware of the different attire brought different reactions in official settings. Hospital visiting, funerals for non-church people and other such settings often meant explanations, many deacons found themselves in awkward situations. One deacon describes how he was asked to identify himself and explain his reason for visiting a sick member of his congregation, only to see a completely unknown minister in clericals breeze through without question. This, and a desire to be identified as a "minster of the church" without awkward explanations seems to have brought a situation where a number of deacons have taken advantage of the permission to wear a dog collar, which was granted for specific conditions, and taken to wearing this as their usual form of dress.

COMMENTS
The paper *What is a Deacon?* notes the problem of understanding of service in today's society and emphasises Thomas Bowman Stephenson's second principle for deaconess formation and behaviour, however, was 'discipline without servility' which they quote from his original *Concerning Sisterhoods* text.

I wrote of this problem in the text of this book in an attempt to bring out the difference in understandings which have been and sometimes are found with the concept of "service ministry". The core of that understanding lies in the difference between a service that is demanded of someone by an employer or superior and the service offered by one person to another without obligation. This is clearly exemplified in the passage from John 13, 12-16. Jesus is not the disciples' servant, but offers them all the service they may need.

Para 5.2 of *What is a Deacon* includes the following explanation of Witness through Service:

For a Methodist deacon, every act of witness (spoken or embodied) is to be exercised as a form of servant ministry, or it becomes an expression of human power or of selfseeking.

Similarly, every act of service is to be exercised as a form of witness, or it becomes a form of servility or an action of merely ethical worth.

For me this last statement has always been of paramount importance. In one of the sermons created for the project I made the point that what I did personally was charity, what I did as an agent of the Church was my *diakona*. The importance of this has been shown to me over and over again throughout my ministry and in interactions with others. There are those who say that the community will not receive them if they come as ministers, and that it is best to dress and speak in the manner of the community if we are to be accepted. Worst of all there are some from the church who say speaking about God is a turn-off and will garner rejection. Our service is "an act of witness". If we are not offering God's mercy, proclaiming the Good news, who are we serving?

In para 6.6 of *What is a Deacon?* there is a discourse on "the Centre" and its value to the Order and to the life of the deacons. The Centre is no more, the building sold and administration and the office of the Warden are now housed in Methodist Church House. This was a loss in practical terms, but also in the spirituality of those deacons for whom this had continued to represent "home" in succession to the Deaconess Houses of the past.

Over the last few years, Faith and Order have discussed and considered the role of Deacons in several aspects of ministry and liturgy. Most of these reflections are available in the Faith and Order papers. Perhaps the most important and relevant to all deacons is the change in our liturgical role. It requires all deacons to fulfill their ministry of witness through leading worship and preaching where appropriate. This change is to include being available for the plan. In the past those of us who were Local Preachers were listed amongst the number in the plan, now wer are listed amongst the ministers. For some circuits at least, this has been taken as a major change and the deacon is no longer seen as a worship leader, but as a leader of worship, there is a real difference in that understanding.

These changes have come about through theological reflection of the role of the diaconate in the Methodist Church, but there is a certain pragmatism at work in light of the spreading difficulties of filling the plan.

As I have described in my story, I was a preaching deacon and originally required to do baptisms weddings and funerals. In a later setting I was banned from these offices, as has been the experience of many deacons. From what I hear on the MDO Facebook page, I suspect that baptisms and funerals are more the norm today.

I have described the deacon's role as plastic, by which I mean we are not bound by rigid images of our role. These new changes are a further example of that plasticity. In my view Methodist Deacons are not bound by a prescribed description of what we do. We are recognized by what we are and have the room to become the minister needed in the appointment to which we are sent.

What follows is the project, its theological reflection and conclusions.

PREFACE

If the average Methodist is unclear about the deacon's ministry this is not surprising. There is little guidance to be found. The Church is much more likely to tell you what deacons do not do than what they do. It can be said that "What does a deacon do?" is not a proper question, but it is the question most people start with and we should be able to offer an answer.

If I was to start: "The deacon's role is to represent the Servant Christ." what would this mean for someone considering diaconal ministry or for a circuit considering the appointment of a deacon? Generally speaking, it would bring about a certain glazing of the eyes or, where someone is prepared to struggle, it would raise many more questions than it answers.

When I offered to candidate for the Order, I asked for some information about the Methodist Diaconal Order (MDO) only to be told that there was no literature. Despite this lack of information about what it meant to be a Methodist Deacon, people had been responding to a call to enter the Methodist Diaconal Order for some six years. They, as I, had a clear sense of call to a *ministry* which was something other than presbyteral.

Congregations considering the appointment of a deacon to their circuit have their own questions: "In what way is a deacon different from a 'minister'?" or when they meet the deacon, "When will you become a proper minister?". The usual answer the church, at whatever level, gives to the first question is that deacons don't "do" communion. The answer I have learned to give to the second is, "I prefer to be an improper minister!" These answers are not really helpful either to the deacon or to the questioner.

In 1996, I was given the opportunity by the Urban Theology Unit at Sheffield to undertake a project to try to discover answers to some of the questions about the role of the deacon. This project, part of the work toward a Master of Ministry and Theology degree, was to be set up with the active cooperation of the congregations which I served. To this end, twelve members of the churches, one community development worker and myself set out on a journey of discovery together which was to involve each of us in a greater commitment than any one of us envisaged at the outset.

My hope is that the reader will end up, not only with an answer to the question "What does a deacon *do*?", but with some understanding of what it means to *be* a deacon.

PART ONE

A SEARCH FOR A MINISTRY

Chapter One

Diaconal Ministry:
A Personal Understanding
and Beginning

I was sent as a probationer deacon to the Castleford circuit in West Yorkshire where I was to work in the housing estates of Airedale, Ferry Fryston and Townville. The application to have a deacon stationed in the circuit said that they wanted 'someone to assist with *the work of the church* in the community'. The job description included pastoral care of the Airedale and Townville churches. I was to assist the community work of these two churches.

By the end of the first year, I had become aware that my expectations and those of the congregations differed. While I was struggling to understand what caused the difference, and how to reconcile it, the opportunity to do an in-depth study of this situation was offered by the Urban Theology Unit. The starting point for the project was an analysis of the situation. My first task was to find out something about this community in which we were to work. The 'we', as I understood it, being myself and the congregations I was to assist.

My view of the community was composed partly of the information presented to me from outside, and partly from the early impressions I had gathered. It seemed to me that I needed to see it from within rather than outside, and a group of people was gathered together who would work with me. These are the people referred to as the 'team', and they were crucial to all that took place. As a team they did not work so much for me as shared in the work with me. It was in discussion with this group and in hearing how they saw the estate that I began to understand the inadequacy of my first external view.

Initially, I had seen a community with problems and a place that was at the bottom of the social ladder in Castleford. The impression I had received from those outside was that this is how it had always been. The conversations with the team made it clear that this was not how those who had lived there for many years saw themselves or their estate. There was a pride in the area, a distinct belief that where they lived, and where they had been brought up, was a good place to live. In fact the parents of most of the group had chosen to live in Airedale. The picture they painted bore little relation to the reputation of the area. What gradually became clear was that this group of seemingly undefined estates was only so to an outsider. To the native, there were distinct divides, and each area bounded by these invisible divides had its own history covering more than seventy years of change and growth. My impression of an ex-mining community was true enough, but only part of the truth.

Discoveries

The team took me through Castleford's industrial history, telling of the clay and sand workings to make bricks for the construction industry and the potteries that were so important in the past. Although fine china manufacture finished in 1961, brick manufacture continued into the 1970s. Glass was manufactured in Castleford from the eighteenth century until 1980 when the closing of the last glass works cost 600 jobs. Hickson's Chemicals is now the largest employer in Castleford. For women in particular the various clothing manufacturers and the confectionery factory, now owned by Nestlé, have been important employers for at least two generations.

What surprised me was that mining was just a memory. Despite the fact that coal has been mined in and around Castleford since the sixteenth century and that the industry grew to be pre-eminent in the whole of the area during the first half of the last century, it is not much talked about. The visual signs are being erased. The mines that shed more than 3,000 jobs in the late eighties, and brought about the loss of 2,000 more in the associated power stations, are now only names on Working Men's Clubs.

The Growing Community

Airedale, Ferry Fryston and Townville are distinct areas of Castleford, a town of some 40,000 people. Castleford, with its long and chequered industrial history, was at the nadir of its economic fortune. Positioned to the east of Leeds and bordered on the north by the river Aire, on the south by the M62 and on the east by the A1, Castleford is best known for its rugby league team. The two Methodist churches with which I worked serve this neighbourhood comprising the Ferry Fryston electoral ward of the Wakefield Metropolitan District Council.

'The estate', to use the term applied to it by council officials and inhabitants alike, which is Airedale, is the result of a rolling building programme over four decades which absorbed the two earlier communities of Airedale and Ferry Fryston into one vast housing development. The neighbouring estate of Townville retains its identity and provides the principal area of private housing within the ward.

Although this was a mining community, it could not be called typical. A short drive around the neighbouring coalfield towns revealed a marked difference between them and Airedale. Airedale was originally developed in the 1920s as a model housing estate which marked it out from the poorer quality housing in neighbouring mining communities. But this bright face was beginning to show the ravages of poverty. Despite the outward differences, the people's history had many similarities to the less attractively designed towns of the neighbouring coalfields.

Airedale was built as a long ribbon development running through what was once Fryston Wood. The growth of the estate coincided with the massive development of the mining industry in the locality. Over four decades, a vast area was covered with housing in four waves of building. This was intended to accommodate the miners who worked in the seven pits directly around the estate. By the 1980s Wheldale pit alone employed nearly 4,000 men. The last development, at the foot of Ferry Fryston, was built to house the workers at the vast Ferrybridge Power Station complex a mile away, which employed 3,400 men.

Many of the older people can remember hard times in the days before the Second World War when their fathers were laid off without pay, or their wages were reduced without notice. In the years after the war things changed and Airedale became a place of high employment with good incomes. Men were hard working, hard drinking, and usually involved in cricket or rugby league. They were members of their trade union and their politics would be almost solidly socialist. The women did all the work in the home. Single women and a minority of the married women worked in the local sweet factory, in clothing factories locally or in Leeds. They did not belong to trade unions. Most women attended church or chapel. If women had political views, they could not express them in front of their menfolk and at home they were expected to keep their mouths shut when the men were talking. Although this is a generalisation, it is the picture painted by the older women to whom I talked about this period.

By the time of the miners' strike of 1984/85 employment at the mines was being seriously eroded and by 1991 when the last Castleford pit closed, there was no turning back of the clock. The power stations also were 'rationalising' their staff and today there are only about 370 employed in the whole Ferrybridge complex.

The Redundancy Factor

It took two years for me to understand the real situation on the estates. The initial impression given was that the problems were those of the unemployed miners and power station workers. It was the way it was always stated. The reality was subtly different.

Over a period of ten to twelve years these work places shed 80 per cent of their workforce. Pits and power stations ceased to take on new workers from the mid-eighties and at the same time they made the older workers redundant. Layer by layer they shed the upper age groups and those with health problems. Retirement carried on at its usual pace, but no-one was brought in to replace the retiring workforce. By the time the final closures came those employed in the remaining mines and power station were a narrow age band of experienced and skilled men, generally 30–50 year olds. Almost all those who had gone had received a good redundancy package or taken early retirement.

The redundant and retired male workers still lived on the estate. They were moderately comfortable and, if the women in the family could get some part-time work, holidays abroad were very possible. Many of the children of this group were still in their early teens at the time of redundancy and grew up throughout that impressionable period in comfortable homes where no one worked, or worked very little. These were homes where people could still go regularly to the local Miners' Club, drive cars, and have all the modern amenities.

By the mid 1990s, the young people of the estate were faced with no work and decreasing benefits: they expected little more than manual work. Unlike previous generations, the society in which they had been nurtured did not give them a model of 'no work no money', one in which being out of employment meant deprivation. Instead they grew to adulthood at a time when it seemed quite possible to do nothing and still to live comfortably. They were, and are, understandably confused.

The 1991 National Census figures showed that 45.9 per cent of the households in this community had no one in employment. This was nearly 25 per cent above the figure for the Metropolitan District of Wakefield as a whole.

For the young people of this area, employment prospects could not have been worse. In the twenty to twenty-four years old age band only 55 per cent were in work while 2.1 per cent were students. For those in the sixteen to nineteen-year age group, with 25.7 per cent registered out of work and a further 9 per cent not in work but no longer on the register, things looked bleak. Whilst in the District as a whole 32.5 per cent of this age group were in further education, the figure for our community was only 21.8 per cent.

Other Social Factors

Historically education has not had a high profile among the people of the Airedale estate. Anecdotal evidence suggests that before the Second World War grammar school places were not available for the young people from this estate. The reason given by one woman was that they were needed down the mines. If young men had been given educational opportunities, they would not have been willing to go into the pits. She was adamant that many young men of promise and intelligence were refused educational opportunity on these grounds. This perception has led to a closed community where leaving to go to higher education is almost unthinkable. The low uptake of higher education in the area and work amongst young people by the Chrysalis Youth Project[1] has led to a recent attempt to solve this problem by introducing new training opportunities within the estate.

Other social factors affected the community and resulted in deprivation amongst the young people, e.g.[2]

- 5.4 per cent of children are on the child protection register compared with 1.7 per cent in the District.
- Births to women under the age of 19 are 27.3 per cent compared with 10.3 per cent in the District.
- 59 per cent of all households receive some form of housing benefit and 42 per cent of tenants are in rent arrears.
- School absenteeism in Airedale is 10 per cent whilst in the District as a whole it is 6.6 per cent
- 45.3 per cent of households are without a car whilst in the District this figure is 38.2 per cent
- Only 42 per cent of homes in Airedale are owner-occupied compared with 61 per cent District wide.

According to a recent survey the use of drugs, particularly injectable drugs (i.e. heroin), was increasing at an alarming rate. Perhaps one of the most disturbing figures was the indication that sharing of needles was up to seven times more common within the Airedale estate compared with the District as a whole, with 77.7 per cent of those surveyed admitting to some needle sharing. The health hazards in such a situation speak for themselves.[3]

The high concentration of this sort of problem amongst the younger generation, and the process by which it has come about, were not unique. What was important was that the perspectives of young people in such a situation were not those of the generation who govern and who make the rules. Memories of struggle and hard times for the older generations were memories of a community rising from the bottom into the light of hope. The young, however, had memories of plenty, of comfort and a good standard of living which had not disappeared, and to which they themselves aspired.

Where does the Church fit in?

I) Townville

The first of the churches to come into being was the Townville Church. In 1911 Townville was a garden suburb of Castleford, built by a man called John Townend. The housing was good with large gardens and designed for the professional classes.

A Primitive Methodist society was formed first on September 27th of that year and met first in the Townville Recreation room. At that meeting the collection and teas raised £3 5s 4d with which they purchased an organ, a pulpit bible, twelve bibles, account books and Sunday School Hymn Books. The Society met there until November 1919 when the church was built. The whole building cost £850. It was the eighth church in the Primitive Methodist Circuit of Castleford at that time and was capable of seating 150 people. At the opening Mr Thwaite, one of the Trustees, was reported to be 'glad that they had not put 'Primitive Methodist Church' over the door as he looked forward to the day when there would be a Methodist Church of England.'[44]. This was extremely forward looking since Methodist Union was not achieved until 1932 and the Primitive and Wesleyan circuits in Castleford remained separate until 1954.

The church flourished and in the 1950s a new Coal Board estate was built at the other end of the road, Gypsy Lane, which increased Sunday School numbers significantly. At this time the Sunday School met in a wooden hut in the church grounds and it was decided to build a hall, extending the original building. This project was completed in 1961 at a cost of £6,580. The new hall included a stage and this was put to good use on the formation of a strong drama group. The church thrived in the 1960s and there was an active youth group, the drama group along with a strong Boys' Brigade and Girls' Brigade. The church was the centre of social activity for Townville at the time and was the significant meeting place for the young people of the day.

The bright young Methodists of the late sixties are the congregation of today. There are two or three members from the seventies Girls' Brigade and then no more young people staying on.

From the latter half of the seventies, until the beginning of the nineties, the Sunday School thrived and the Brigades did well. They served the Coal Board estate from which children were sent, but parents never came. The demolition of that estate in 1993 spelled the end for the Sunday School and removed the congregation's raison d'etre. The 'Mums and Toddlers' group is the one sign of service to the community that the Townville church has left. It is in great demand and is run entirely as a service by a group of women from the Church. Although it has been operating for a number of years there is no sign that anyone from the community has offered, or would offer, to assist in the running of the group. No one from the Mums and Toddlers has come into the family of the church although in the last year we have had two baptisms from it.

ii) Airedale

The Airedale estate had its beginnings in 1922 when the first segment of the development was begun. The local council planned to build the new housing with a government grant which was available at the time. Then the government suddenly gave a finishing date for all housing under the scheme. The council was made of stern stuff and told the builders that if the whole scheme were not completed on time there would be no payment. The scheme was completed in record time and the government paid up. The new housing ran in a long strip down through what had been woodland and part of the Fryston estate. It was intended to be, and certainly was seen as, model housing. There was great competition to be housed in Airedale at that time.

Although on a modern street map Airedale and Townville are seen to merge into one another and you can walk from Townville Church to Airedale Church in fifteen minutes, it was not so in 1922. The connecting road, Poplar Avenue, was not built for nearly twenty years, although a footpath came into being in the 1930s.. This meant that the two communities had little contact with each other at that time.

In 1922 a group of the new tenants in Airedale came together to form a Methodist Society. Perhaps the fact that they were Wesleyans added to the distance from the other Methodist Societies in the immediate area. They were able to obtain a piece of land in Fryston Road on which stood the canteen hut of the workmen who had built the estate. The hut became the first meeting place and went on to serve the church for sixty-seven years, first as the church until the present church was built in 1929, and then as a Sunday School until it was demolished in 1989. When it was built the woods still bordered the building site. It was not until ten years later that the junction on which it now stands appeared, when the original estate was extended and the Ferry Fryston development was completed.

In Airedale too, the Church became a social centre, with a drama group, choir, Boys' Brigade and Girls' Brigade. The Sunday School was also well attended and memories linger on of huge congregations and banked seating for Sunday School anniversaries. Whereas Townville was at its height in the sixties, numbers at Airedale had already slumped and was noted in circuit reports 'as giving concern for its survival'. By the early seventies the Girls' Brigade and the Boys' Brigade had both closed down and Sunday School numbers fell to an all-time low. At this time it was not uncommon to have congregations of as few as eight or nine people.

One of the oldest members of the present congregation suggests that things were never the same after the war. He says that many of the young men who survived the war and had been part of the church never came back to Airedale. Those who did were so changed that they rarely came back to the church.

During most of the 1950s and 1960s Airedale and Townville were served by a succession of Pastors, a form of lay ministry which Methodism employed for some time after the war. Those who remembered described some of them as 'odd'. Airedale's problems continued to grow. One minister who served the circuit in the 1970s can remember an occasion when he turned up for a service and only one young girl turned up. The church was not even opened. Whatever was happening, the service to the community must have been negligible. It was not until the 1980s that a new spark of life came into the congregation.

A new minister in the circuit, Janet Mackinder, seems to have been one of the factors in this renewal, and there was also a small infusion of new blood at this time. By the mid 1980s the plan to rebuild the Church Hall was in hand and a fundraising campaign was under-way. By 1989 when the old hut was demolished to make way for the new building, things were much more alive. In 1986 the chapel at Glasshoughton had closed and the Girls' Brigade company had moved to Castleford bringing a renewal of youth work.

In 1989 the first deacon, Glenda Sidding, was stationed in the circuit with special responsibilities in Airedale and Townville. The extra attention came at the right time. The building of the new hall was just beginning and the renewed activity could be fostered more directly. In 1991 a new captain restarted the Boys' Brigade which gave further impetus to the Sunday School.

Once the hall was completed the deacon encouraged a group of women from the congregation to reach into the community through the provision of a lunch club and a Saturday coffee morning and a mini-market. Their vision was one of offering a meeting-place for those who were alone at home, and an opportunity for the poorer families on the estate to buy good second-hand clothes.

The Deacon's story – (1) A long journey

In 1994 I was a 'bright new probationer deacon', fresh out of college. I was also 55 years old. The bright new probationer was sprouting from a lifetime of experience, much of it to do with church.

I was brought up in Edinburgh and attended a school where religious education was taken by a minister of the Kirk. That was my total direct education in such matters, plus some history taught with a strong Scottish content, including the history of the Church of Scotland. At home there was no connection with the church in any way, and I was not baptized until I came to consider marriage.

My first significant experience of church was in Bridgnorth as a National Service airman. I was offered the chance of a night out, a time away from camp. The fact that it involved a church service before the social was irrelevant to all of the young men who went that night. It was a Baptist Church and I have no memory of the social which attracted me. Yet the whole experience has left a lasting memory which has stayed with me for thirty-seven years. A memory of a gathering of people who were at ease with themselves, who put us at ease and did so for no hope of gain or advantage for themselves or their organisation. The young airmen whom they welcomed every month were passing through and could not be expected ever to return. We were welcomed into their family for that short time and made to feel a part of it. That short evening visit left me with a sense of community and welcome that changed my whole view of the church.

At twenty years of age, with my marriage to a church member in view, I became a member of the Church of Scotland at the local church and in the years following National Service became, first a Scout leader, and later an ordained elder. Without my experience at Bridgnorth, I would have simply replied 'No thank you' when I was asked to take on the role of elder. Instead, I took it seriously and asked a friend who was a minister to explain the role more fully. My ordination into that role is still important to me.

Within a few years I had moved south with my family to East Anglia and we joined the local Congregational Church where we happily worshipped for the next seven years. My time in the Congregational church seems to have left little mark on me despite making several lasting friendships.

In 1974 my work took us to Mid-Wales and a different church. This time I settled into a comfortable, old-fashioned low Methodist setting, gradually becoming more involved as steward, circuit steward and then training as a local preacher. I was 40 when I became a circuit steward, with no idea what the post really involved. Yet those seven years as a circuit steward prepared me for ministry and taught me the meaning of Methodism. I was involved more and more deeply with, and working for, the Church in a number of areas. This involvement led to suggestions from friends, ministerial and lay, that I should consider the ministry. Being a 'minister', a presbyter (although I had not encountered the term at this time), did not seem right to me. I had heard about the Methodist Diaconal Order[5] (MDO) at the Methodist Conference in 1989 and when my superintendent minister asked me to attend a 'Ministries Day' in Birmingham in 1992 where the MDO was included, I accepted. Out of that day came my candidature to the Order.

If I was wholeheartedly a Methodist, my feet were nonetheless still solidly placed in the Church of Scotland. With a background like that one might wonder how I came to feel called to a religious order and an order of ministry which I had barely encountered and of which I had had no experience.

Without ever directly asking the question 'Why a religious order', I began to find answers throughout my training. In every sector of my studies connections were made, but not emphasized, and it was not until others asked the question, 'In what way is this a different ministry?', that I began to try to find answers to offer them.

There is nothing in my faith journey that suggests that I would feel a call to a religious life, but it exists. Belonging to the community of the MDO has become important to me as a person, and the shared spirituality supports my faith.

There is a sense in which I feel that if the Order had not existed then I would have had to invent it!

Diaconal ministry is another matter. I have for a long time held a very high view of the sacrament of Holy Communion. For me the essence of communion is sharing. The sharing with God and the sharing with my fellow worshippers is what I value. For me it seemed right to receive the elements of bread and wine in company with the church community. Aware of the great privilege of presiding, I still did not feel called to enter that particular office. Although, as a local preacher, I had become accustomed to lead worship, I did not feel that this should be the focus of my Christian service either. The deacon's ministry seemed to offer the possibility to serve in a way that would overcome my lack of call to a sacramental ministry. It seems that there are some who come into the Order with a sense of calling only to the diaconal ministry, and no calling to belong to an Order. For myself one is as important as the other. In the Methodist Council's 1997 Report to Conference it states 'No candidate should therefore be ordained to diaconal ministry in Methodism, who will not gladly belong to the Order.'[6] This had been assumed, but not stated, in the previous ten years. The conversations in groups at Convocation[7] over the past few years had revealed that not every deacon would concur with this.

As I look back there are questions to be answered which I never thought to ask myself at the time. These questions have taken me onto the path of discovery and form the basis of this project. My journey to this point has been a lengthy one, each step having to build on the previous one. Now, the project experience has offered me an opportunity to understand my sense of calling more fully.

I have been asked if I started this project to discover what it meant to be a deacon. There is some truth in that. Perhaps more accurately, I set out to find out how to be a deacon and then to explain this to those denominations that were ordaining deacons. It was the 'how to be' with which I was struggling. Even as I write new insights come to light, and I find a need to incorporate these insights into my thinking.

All of the above is to do with my church connection and, if I left it at that, it would be possible to assume that my life had been church-centred. This would be far from the truth. The bulk of my life experience has been in my secular employment.

I served my apprenticeship in the printing industry as a typesetter (compositor) in the Scotsman Publications in Edinburgh starting at fifteen years old. After making an early marriage and completing my National Service I moved out of *The Scotsman* and went South. There my work was on a shift basis and payment was through a bonus system with unsocial hours and pressure to perform. Although I continued to attend church, my life was really focused on work. The move to Mid-Wales was to another printing firm where I eventually became production manager. During twenty years in Mid-Wales I changed jobs twice, always involving high pressure and long hours. For most of this time my work was my life. I had no thought of ministry other than to wonder if the minister's sermon would send me to sleep on Sunday if I was not working and got to church at all.

My first step out of this scenario was at a garden party when I asked my minister, 'Is there something I could do for the church'. It was nearly as big a surprise to him as it was to me for I had acted on a sudden impulse. He asked me to become a circuit steward, which I accepted. Within three years I had given up my employment and taken on a less time-consuming job developing a small local wholesale and retail company which allowed more time for serving the church. At that time my wife and I started to work voluntarily as circuit missioners, working alongside a minister to bring a programme of mission to the churches of the circuit. Twelve months after taking that first step I offered for diaconal ministry.

The Deacon's Story – (2) An Alien Sort Of Levite

I arrived in Castleford in August 1994 feeling sure that I understood diaconal ministry and that I could live it out in the situation facing me. I felt fortunate that the churches had had a deacon in the post before me. Glenda[8] had been there for three years and I had been told that she had developed work in the community and within the church. The circuit statement, which described the expectations and the format for the appointment indicated a good understanding of diaconal ministry. It was therefore reasonable to assume that I would have few difficulties in being a deacon. I was looking forward to the challenge of establishing how I should fit into the work in progress and find a particular focus for my own ministry.

My welcome service was fitting and supportive, and seemed to offer a liturgical framework for the deacon's ministry. The welcome supper at Airedale Church sounded no wrong notes. It made me smile that a couple of weeks after arrival an elderly lady introduced me as 'the new vicar'. I assumed it was merely a local idiosyncrasy and thought little more of it. Gradually I came to realize that this was not the case. Although a comparatively few people used the term, I was often introduced as 'the new minister'. Within Airedale particularly, if not as much in Townville, I was seen as the minister. It was as their leader, administrator and pastor that they understood my ministry.

I was a stranger in a foreign country where the people wanted to make the deacon acceptable. It was not a rejection of what I am, it was simply that 'what I am' is not a recognisable persona. A deacon no more fits into the world they know than a rhinoceros fitted the world of the ancient Greeks. The rhinoceros was understood as a horse with a horn (a unicorn); the deacon seems to be understood as a minister without the authority to preside at communion. I came to realize that what had happened to my predecessor was that, as time went on, the pressure of expectation had changed her perception of herself until she felt that she had been given a call to eucharistic ministry and went on to candidate for presbyteral ministry. If I was not to allow the pressures to change me in the same way I needed to understand not only what a deacon is, with total clarity, but how to be a deacon in a world where they are not recognized.

The lack of comprehension was probably most clearly seen on the face of my Anglican colleague who came to visit me soon after I had settled in. He had had a good working relationship with my predecessor, unsure of her status within either her church or his, but happy to see her as a deaconess and to co-operate with her. What was quite clear on his first visit was that he felt that some of his difficulties were now a thing of the past. I was a man and therefore would, presumably, become a fully-fledged minister in time. Meantime I could be understood as some sort of curate. When he was told that I would be a permanent deacon and that I had never intended anything else, he could not understand the 'How' or the 'Why'. Being something of a pragmatist he seemed to decide that the mysteries of Methodism were beyond him and he simply treated me as a colleague.

My difficulty with the congregations at Airedale and Townville was that I had to help them to see the rhinoceros and recognize that both horses and rhinoceroses existed in their world. For the congregation this meant that they needed to accept the alien deacon for himself/herself and not to attempt to integrate him/her into their own understanding of ministry until there was no discernible difference.[9]

Opening Understandings

I was accepted for training for the MDO in March 1993. In June of that year the Conference[10] received a report from the Faith and Order Committee which addressed the issue 'Deacons and deaconesses either belong to an order of ministry, theologically comparable to the diaconate in the churches which have a three-fold ministry, or they do not' The report was only the start of a process which has gone on until the present day. The defining paragraph of the report says: 'Deacons and deaconesses are a "focus".'

There is not within Methodism an obvious process for such a theological discussion or decision. Conference, which makes decisions in such matters, is not constructed in such a way, nor given time, to allow it to consider complex theological matters.

Chapter Two

Social Realities
and Local Expectations

Introduction

Perhaps I would have simply pushed aside my questions concerning diaconal ministry and learned to work within the situation in which I found myself if I had not decided to undertake a project. Possibly I would have found myself carrying out the role into which I was being pushed, only questioning it when in the company of other deacons, such as Convocation. Obviously it was not a new situation, as I had heard deaconesses from the old Wesley Deaconess Order tell similar stories in the past, but I thought there had to be a better way to deal with this misapprehension. People were still coming into the Order and many other denominations were talking about diaconal ministry. Here was an opportunity to look at my situation with those involved within it and together respond to some of the questions that were in people's minds.

How had I come to be invited to do a job with a set of expectations that were not those of the people with whom I would work? Was it possible to establish the real needs of the people whom I was to serve and to respond to them within the role to which I was called?

It seemed likely that working as a group would be the best process for examining the situation of the local church and their understandings of ministry. This offered an opportunity to produce an overview of the church and its relationships and to determine where the problem lay. With this in mind, a number of people from both churches were asked if they would be willing to be involved in this way. From an initial list of eighteen, thirteen people agreed to be part of the group (referred to throughout this book as 'the team'). We would be clarifying our own perceptions and trying to come to an understanding of the various expectations and needs. Through this process it was hoped that we would be able to suggest a suitable way to respond.

Companions on the Journey

The team met for the first time at Airedale Methodist Church on 24 July 1996. It was an opportunity to explain why we were there, what I hoped we would do and to ask people to undertake specific tasks. I suggested that it was only possible to create a true picture if we had sufficient information about our situation and so this would be a key task. The history of the churches and the estates was of primary importance and two members of the team were able to offer particular help in this. A member from Townville, not on the team, shared her collection of historical information about the churches. The non-church member was to be particularly helpful on the social aspects of the area and in evaluating the work we would undertake. Our present and past circuit stewards helped us with the wider expectation of the circuit, whilst those from the two local churches kept us focused on immediate needs.

At the suggestion of one of the team (Jeannette Woodhead), I asked Mike Dixon to chair the meetings. This proved to be a wise suggestion. Mike chaired meetings well without attempting to apply his own agenda, while maintaining good control of a varied group and their different agendas. Looking back over the records of the meetings one can see the contribution that each member made. There were surprises and, inevitably, some could not give as much time as others, but the group worked well together, gave me tremendous support, and made possible things that would otherwise have been difficult to achieve. Our non-church participant[1] was patient with the devotional aspect of each meeting and dealt with the need for theology with equanimity.

Interestingly the non-theologically-trained members of the team had least trouble with the term 'theology' and simply worked with the material. Some of the most telling theological questions came from them.

Our meetings always started with coffee/tea and biscuits and with prayer. Most meetings had a bible study. All had a reporting and a reflection time. I was immensely supported by the efforts which others have into this work, some sitting back quietly at times and at others leading the discussion.

Introducing the Team

The team I describe are those who met and worked with me during 1996–98. I have been able to keep in touch with all but Jeanette. I hope they will understand that I speak of them in the past tense because situations change and life will have moved on for them. By now their involvement will be different but these are the people who shared this journey with me.

Mike Dixon was a member of Airedale Church where he was property steward and Boys' Brigade Captain. Although he had only been a member at Airedale for about six years, having come into the area from another circuit, he had put a tremendous commitment into the church and the Boys' Brigade. It was not his family's first connection with the church at Airedale. His father was one of the early members and is still remembered by many of the older members with affection. Mike, a school caretaker when the project started, worked at a special school in the area where he had been instrumental in creating a close relationship between the church and the school. He was involved with several community groups. Despite my concern that I might be over- stretching him, he very willingly accepted when I asked him.

Maureen Dean was a circuit steward and a member at Townville Methodist Church. Maureen had taken early retirement from being an infant school teacher a few years previously. She was one of the leaders of the Mums and Toddlers group at Townville and was also the regular organist. Along with a good knowledge of the present situation in the circuit and a long involvement in circuit and local church affairs, Maureen brought a sharp enquiring mind to the project. She proved to be one of the most consistent partners in the team, gently challenging if I tried to impose my own agenda.

John Dean is Maureen's husband and a local preacher. John was the property steward and treasurer at Townville church as well as sharing with Maureen the organ- playing duties. He also took early retirement from being a primary school headmaster. Meeting times often unavoidably clashed with John's choir practice nights and this meant that he could not be very regular in attendance. Despite an undoubted difference of theological and ecclesiological approach between John and myself, his support was unstinting and valued.

Alison Drake was also a member at Townville Chapel. Alison was head teacher of a primary school until a serious fall left her very incapacitated and unable to continue work. Alison is intelligent and erudite with an interest in the theological as well as the practical side of church work. Alison found evening meetings too tiring and she had to withdraw from the team. Her ongoing interest and support made her a valuable consultant to me.

Margaret Gill was Airedale's Sunday School Superintendent. Margaret was in her late forties, very active in church affairs and interested in circuit matters. She was one of the keenest members of the Bible Study groups. She worked as a full-time Library assistant, and had two daughters, one of whom had just completed training as a deacon in the Methodist Diaconal Order. Margaret's husband was a postal worker and for her to give up regular evenings was a considerable commitment. Her knowledge of Airedale was particularly helpful, as were her insights into the problems of ministry.

Edna Holmes was in her late seventies and a widow. She had been an active part of the church and community in Airedale most of her life. She was a church steward for four years and acted as reserve steward at the time of the project. She was treasurer of the Ladies' Bright Hour, occasional speaker and reserve chairperson. Edna was the surprise of the group for me, with her quick responses and participation in the discussions.[2]

Irene Kelly was in her mid-forties, and a recent member of the church. She had become a pastoral visitor and a door steward, was involved in the community work of the church and edited the church magazine, and worked in the office of a local manufacturer. Since joining the team Irene had become a church steward and her confidence had grown apace. Like Edna, Irene was something of a surprise. Seemingly diffident and shy at first, she became forceful in debate and offered important insights. Her need to express things often put real meat on the bones of a discussion. Perhaps because she was younger in the life of the church, she tended to ask the awkward questions.

John McCarthy was the Superintendent Minister of the circuit and Minister in Charge of the two churches that were in my care. John was fifty-nine at the time we started and had served in the Castleford circuit for ten years. He was keen to be involved in the project but other pressures meant that he gradually withdrew from the group, although he kept in touch with what was happening. It was John's vision that had brought a diaconal appointment to the circuit, so it was a pity we lost his background knowledge.

Lynda Seabury, a member at Townville Chapel, was the wife of a miner and a pastoral visitor of considerable care and commitment. She had undergone the theory part of the local preachers training without feeling a call to preach. Her knowledge of theology was extensive and she still kept up her reading. Her theological stance was not the same as mine but we could happily agree to differ.

Dorothy Townend (Dot) who was seventy years old, was very active in the community work of the church at Airedale and as a pastoral visitor. She had recently become a church steward. The widow of a miner, she had worked in a clothing factory and done office work. Although Dot had been a regular attender for more than twenty years she had only been made a member in the last twelve months. Of all those on the team, she was perhaps the most familiar with the work I did in the community. Dot was involved in all the kitchen work in the church, the lunch clubs, the coffee mornings and the funeral teas. There were not many days when she was not in the church and her views on why we were doing what we were doing were invaluable.

Peter Wadsworth was in his fifties, an ex-mining engineer who at the time of starting the project worked for Wakefield Metropolitan Council, but later had to take early retirement owing to chronic arthritis. He had recently retired as circuit steward and taken on the post of church steward at Airedale where he was also church treasurer. Peter was heavily involved in the local history society. His contribution on the historical front, along with that of his wife, was extremely helpful and Peter's involvement with the diaconal appointment, first as Circuit Steward, and then as Church Steward, working closely with the deacon, had meant that he had a very useful overview. It was from Peter that I often got echoes of the circuit's early vision of a diaconal ministry.

Christine Wadsworth was in her early forties and married to Peter. She was Airedale's Cradle Roll Secretary and a Librarian at Castleford Library. She had a long family relationship with the church at Airedale. Christine was secretary of the Castleford Historical Society and was helpful in providing access to statistical and historical records both of the area and the church.

Jeanette Woodhead was the one member of the team with no church connections. Much of my community involvement was through the Interagency Group in Airedale. Barnardo's W.A.Y. Project, in which Jeanette was a team leader, had facilitated this group. She joined the team because of the community aspects of my work and to give an external perspective. Jeanette was particularly useful in helping the team work through the questions and problems arising and she led the team through the evaluation of my ministry and the time scales involved. Despite her lack of any church background and declared agnosticism, it was Jeanette who often followed through the theological arguments and enabled others to understand them. During the project she changed employment but still continued to give her contribution and full support.

These are the people who worked through the stages of exploring my ministry situation with me. Together we explored the history of the church and the estate, hoping to come to a greater understanding of its mission. I learned with them what the vision of the Church in Airedale was when the first deacon was appointed. We have all been surprised, in different ways, when we looked back at what the circuit officers offered as a vision ten years previously, and what had happened to it since then.

Sharing Memories

The meetings took place in the new church hall, which had the space and facilities we needed.

I led the first meeting and explained how we might work together and what we might achieve. Mike Dixon agreed to chair subsequent meetings. From the first invitation to join the group several of the women had expressed concern about their suitability for the task. As time went by these fears disappeared, but at the first meeting I wanted to give them a paradigm which might be helpful to them. I chose as the Bible reading Luke 8.3 and 24.9–10, introducing Joanna and the women who supported Jesus and who were the first witnesses of the resurrection.

I took the team through the questions that would need to be answered if we were to get to understand the area better. We divided up the work with each person having some part of the analysis to undertake. Peter and Christine agreed to bring back maps of the area with the bus stops, shops and medical services marked and some indication of the development of the estate. Others would look at the church community and its make-up and all were prepared to talk about the estate as their home and what they felt about it.

The second meeting took the form of a meal and discussion. I cooked and served a meal for all the team members and we talked informally over the table about the past, both of the Church and the estate. It was in the discussion at that meeting that many of the questions were raised which were to be important to the work that followed. Just as importantly, I was shown a completely different image of the area than I had hitherto encountered. Some of the issues that I was able to see more clearly after this discussion included:

- Perceptions of the area - my own, those of outsiders and of the team.
- Expectations regarding the deacon - where these came from and the need to clarify them for myself and for others.

- The story of the appointment of a deacon (this had not been heard by all of the team) and the different understandings within the church.
- Questions about what had made the church come alive again and how this could be continued.

To my surprise the prevailing response of the team to questions about the estate as a place to live in was of a good place, a happy neighbourhood in which most of them felt rooted. This contrasted with the ugly picture of deprivation, vandalism, and high rates of crime that I had been given by others, mostly outsiders. The estate had a 'reputation', and there was some truth in these descriptions, but it was a long way from the whole story.

Those who had lived in Airedale from its beginnings, or were part of the families who had come in the early days, remembered a model estate and good neighbours. These had been upright working-class folk and they still associated with the same neighbours they had in the beginning, even though they were now scattered all over the estate or were living in the groups of warden-managed bungalows built in recent times. Some came from the families responsible for the building of the church. This close community feeling which had obviously been the prevailing ethos of the estate in the past was no longer so apparent. What had been a closeness had become a 'closedness'. What had once been a caring and sharing community was now joined only by their rejection by the rest of the town. The feeling one got was of a community with no sense of togetherness, but a sense of being on the 'outside'.

One of the old centres of the community had been Park Dale. Dot Townend told how, in 1954, she was asked to move by the council housing department and did not wish to do so. The housing manager came to see her and explained that the area had been selected for slum clearance and all the early families were being moved out. Reluctantly Dot moved. Park Dale became, and has remained a sink area. This part of the estate, which had been home for many of the older church members when they were younger, was remembered fondly. No one from the church community lives there any longer and the area had become a byword for criminal activity, vandalism and drug abuse. Few people live there for long and the council has seemed to operate a policy of dumping problem families in Park Dale. At the time we were looking at this, one of the leading drug suppliers in the district was arrested in the Park Dale area. The police had targeted him because of the large number of burglaries done by his customers. One young man, only sixteen, whom they arrested at the time, was convicted of seventy-two burglaries.

The Ferry Fryston estate was built in the fifties to house the workers at the Electricity Generating Station at Ferrybridge. This development nearly doubled the original estate in size and population. There was a site designated on the original plans for a new Church, but it was never built. This raised the question of the relationship of the church with the newer parts of the estate. Was there in fact any relationship with the newer parts, or had outreach simply not happened? With the aid of Jeanette Woodhead a questionnaire was devised, which, it was hoped, would give us some indication of where the church congregation originated and when people had come into the church.

The results of the questionnaire were illuminating and gave clues as to why the circuit appointed a deacon to these churches. The questionnaire did indeed show that there had been little or no outreach into the community since the early days with few new adults coming into the church. More importantly it very clearly indicated that the most common route of entry to the church had been through the Girls' and Boys' Brigades. There were one or two exceptions, but the overwhelming impression was of a regular trickle of new members coming through the Brigades.

Margaret Gill had brought to the same meeting a piece of research she had done based on her 40 years association with the Sunday School and the records she had as Sunday School Superintendent. This showed a thriving and successful Sunday School in the fifties and early sixties which coincided with the presence of the Brigades. When the Brigades disappeared, the numbers attending the Sunday School fell sharply. It was not until the return of the Girls' Brigade and its subsequent establishment in the area that the numbers increased again. In 1990 there was an increase of 30 per cent. The life of the church seemed to be linked quite effectively with the life of the Brigades. This link was further evidenced anecdotally by the number of times I heard people, whom I was visiting for funerals, tell of how one or other of their family belonged to the Girls' Brigade, or played an instrument in the Boys' Brigade band. This could not have been the only factor for growth, for although many people had identified either Girls' Brigade or Boys' Brigade as their first contact with the church, these were mainly older people who had come into the church during the first cycle of Brigade activity[3].

The activity and attendance of the church, in the period from the latter half of the sixties until the early eighties, were so poor that there had been moves on the part of the circuit to close the church in Airedale. Although there were few complaints about the ministers that they had during this time, a significant factor in the rebirth of the church seems to have been attributable to the changes made by one minister in particular. Many people have spoken of the spiritual change that came into the life of the church while Janet Mackinder was their minister from 1980 until 1986. Peter and Christine returned to membership of Airedale church at this time through her influence. Questions to the congregation revealed a number of people of all ages who had returned to the church during this period. It was the 'increase in spirituality' that had been important to them. Although many of the activities that enlivened the congregation, and connected it to the community outside were rooted in this period, they were sure that it was not the activity, but the spiritual change which had attracted them. It seemed that the activity and the new life were related to a sense of spirituality which had been absent until that time in a way they could not explain. While people found it difficult to be specific it seemed to me that what they had valued was a spiritual dimension to all that they did; the building work, the extension of community service and particularly a new-found commitment to charitable giving.

The building of the new hall had been 'an activity' that had increased the contribution of many people to the church life. Some had come back to help with the fund raising and had stayed on to be part of the congregation again. Others had begun to put a commitment into the work of the church through the Saturday coffee mornings and the lunch clubs which they would not have offered in any other way. The sense of ownership that comes with contributing seems to have been important to their commitment in the rest of church life. But, whoever I spoke to, it was a feeling of an enhanced spirituality which they gave as the reason for their continuing activity in the church. It is important to note that there are those, within the church, who see some activity as simply fund-raising to maintain the church and tend to look down on it. They are seldom those heavily involved with the particular 'activity'. Those who are involved, seldom speak of it as fund-raising, for them it is the community outreach which is important and the raising of funds is incidental to the activity.

Discerning the Problem – Working Through Confusion

The appointment of a deacon in 1989 was intended to stimulate activity relating to community needs. The deacon's appointment was seen as central to the mission of the church and to a process that would reawaken purpose in the congregations. The circuit had, in fact, sought to make the appointment in 1988 but there were no deacons available at that time.

After Janet Mackinder left the circuit things slowed down a little, By now there were only two ministers for nine churches and the ability to maintain the work was slipping from their grasp.[4] The circuit ministers and stewards decided that they should ask the Connexion to appoint a deacon to the circuit. There was no possibility of keeping three ministers with falling numbers in the circuit, and the shortage of circuit ministers available made this even more certain. The Methodist Diaconal Order stations deacons in situations which can demonstrate a need for this particular style of ministry and in 1989 the circuit was successful in its application and a deacon was sent to take up the appointment. One of the key statements in the application was that the deacon should be responsible 'for taking the churches' work forward with a view to developing that work in the community'.

At this time it was said that the deacon should not have sole pastoral charge of Airedale and Townville Churches but should be working alongside the minister based at Kippax. The deacon, Glenda Sidding, was a probationer who was able to offer experience in youth work and outreach. Glenda became involved in a number of circuit ventures rather than particular church-based projects. There was a circuit youth group that she took under her wing and, although not the full-time leader of the group, she gave it considerable attention and became associated with it in a fairly high-profile way. She also shared in the training of Sunday School teachers with a lay person in the circuit. Each of these was seen as part of her role as a member of the circuit staff working alongside the presbyteral ministers[5].

In 1991 the circuit made the decision to realign the circuit staffing. This coincided with the Methodist Church's decision that deacons should receive the same stipend as presbyters. It was decided that the circuit would find the additional cost, but that the minister at Kippax would withdraw from the Airedale/Townville pastoral situation. This changed the deacon's situation in two ways. Technically a deacon cannot be in pastoral charge of a group of churches; there has to be a presbyter who will preside at church councils. This task fell to the superintendent but in practical terms, for all day-to-day purposes, the deacon was in pastoral charge. The second change was in the perceptions of the congregations and of the deacon around this new role. She was no longer working *alongside* a minister, but was *in place of* a minister. In whatever way the church expressed it, this was how those involved perceived the situation, and it affected their responses. One of the ways in which this changed the situation was that the deacon withdrew, to some extent, from the circuit posts that she had undertaken and concentrated more of her energies in the churches that were now her responsibility. The change in focus had an effect upon Glenda also. As more and more of her work was that of replacing the missing presbyter she began to take on that role and, in 1993, Glenda decided to offer herself to the Church as a candidate for presbyteral ministry. In this Glenda had the wholehearted support of the congregations whom she was serving and who, by this time, were easing her more and more certainly into that role. Glenda's candidature meant that she had to be withdrawn from the post and another deacon appointed in her place.[6]

In 1994 I came to Airedale to replace Glenda as deacon and received the same message from the circuit that my predecessor had received when she arrived. The appointment involved 'broadening the links already created with the community'; I was to be a link with the local community, enabling the work of the church amongst the people outside its own four walls. Although there were clearly some pastoral facets to the role, these were presented as pastoral care to the wider community including the conduct of baptisms, weddings and funerals. I could well see how these were necessary functions if I were to connect with the community as the church's diaconal minister.

No one had described the earlier circuit-wide role of the previous deacon, nor did I attempt to take on that work. It seemed, from the start, that the role I was being asked to assume was solely in the communities around the two churches to which I was to be attached. Despite the similarity in job descriptions, the situation into which I had come was that of 1991, not that of the original 1989 stationing. By this time there were probably three different sets of expectations in the minds of the church members in the circuit.

Expectations Amongst the Confusion

First, there were the expectations of the circuit. By 'circuit' I mean the eight churches which make up the total group. These expectations still included some form of circuit-wide involvement. The tasks my predecessor had undertaken were no longer visible. The circuit youth group no longer met and for the last two years it had only come together for an annual trip to the Methodist Association of Youth Clubs London Weekend. But the churches had not yet awakened to that reality. The training function, for those working with young people, was no longer part of the deacon's remit and was now in the hands of the lay person who had been trained and qualified for this task. Unaware of the background and of the expectations that had been created in the first two years of the appointment and maintained vestigially until now, I was bound to disappoint many people. This did not become clear until the team started to ask the wider circuit what their expectations of a deacon were. Although I could not change the situation, the situation did affect the responses we received.

Secondly, there were the expectations of the two churches with which I was to work. These expectations had arisen out of the ministry of my predecessor. Airedale, in particular, saw me as a substitute presbyteral minister. Perhaps, in view of their history in which they had experienced a number of lay pastors as substitute presbyters, this was not surprising. The fact that the deacon who had been ministering to them had only been able to work alongside a presbyter for two years and had then found herself acting on her own for the past three years meant that they did not have another model to work with.

Thirdly, there were my own expectations. These were engendered by the way the role had been described to me by the superintendent and the circuit officials. I had assumed that they spoke on the circuit's behalf. Of course they did, but not necessarily on behalf of the individual circuit churches. Naturally, I set out to fulfil the role which had been communicated to me and my own understanding of diaconal ministry. I saw myself as a servant of the Church with a purpose of 'being sent' into the community, sent to represent the church. It was my task to 'enable' the diaconal ministry of the congregation.

There were also the expectations of the local community. At the time of starting the project I had been able to continue much of the work in the community done by my predecessor and to make new connections. This community work was becoming well established. What was not happening was the making of any connection between the congregation and the work being done on their behalf. Some of the initial impetus had been lost, since the congregation had come to focus on the deacon as a substitute presbyter. So, although there was work being undertaken in the community, the initial statement from 1989, about it being the 'church's works' had not been fulfilled as they had no ownership of it.

The frequently asked questions, 'What is a deacon for?' or, 'Why can't you do communion?', showed that the congregation had lost, or failed to grasp, the original vision which had moved the Circuit officers to seek the appointment of a deacon. This loss of vision had resulted in congregations misunderstanding the deacon's role as that of a substitute presbyteral minister. On top of this, there were still circuit officials who had expectations of undefined mission in the community beyond Airedale, and within the circuit there were expectations of a generally increased ministerial input which would be difficult to quantify.

This confusion seemed likely to make it impossible to achieve the original aims with their emphasis on the work in the community alongside a wider circuit role in training, nor would it be possible to fulfil all these inappropriate expectations. Worse still would be to try to fulfil some of them in a way which compromised my understanding of my calling.

The team looked at this situation in the context of the statement of the call contained in the ordination service for a deacon:

A deacon is called
> to assist God's people in worship and prayer;
> to minister Christ's love and compassion;
> to visit and support the sick and suffering
> to seek out the lost and the lonely;
> to interpret to the church the needs and concerns of the world;

and to help those you serve to offer their lives to God.[7]

John McCarthy (Superintendent Minister) asked, 'Could this not also apply to any presbyter? In fact is this not the ministry of the whole people of God?' This is a fairly common response when there is an attempt to define diaconal ministry. At the heart of this response lies a confusion between *diakonia,* service, and *diakonos* the servant or the agent. Kevin Flynn[8] describes it thus: '*Diakonia* is something given in baptism. To be a *diakonos*, however, is to be a focused ministry through which the church is able to give expression to its own *diakonia*.'

In the team discussion Alison Drake saw the deacon as: 'an enabler who has more time to find out and learn about problems and people's needs and who would have time to share them'.

Irene Kelly picked up the idea of 'seeking the lost' and shared with us a recent insight that she had experienced through walking into Airedale one morning. Despite having been brought up in the area, this was the first time in years that she had come into the area on foot. She told us of her impressions of the people she encountered in the Magnet Square. She had thought they looked lost. She was unable to describe precisely what it was that had made her feel this, other than to say that many of them looked as if they were without purpose, direction or hope.

The team discussed for some time how far the deacon was able to be an example to, or a focus of, the *diakonia* of the congregation. John McCarthy regretted 'the failure of this intention'. He felt that to seek out the lost and the lonely had been the vision that the circuit, and he in particular, had had at the inception of the diaconal appointment. He described it as a 'ministry without' rather than a 'ministry within'. He went on to say that he did not think that the church was 'allowing sufficient time for this to happen', that 'there were many demands made on the deacon's time and that this limited what could be done'.

Clarifying the Problem

Until this distinction, between diaconal and presbyteral ministry, was made clear neither the congregation nor the deacon would be able to see the circuit's vision for this post clearly. It would be easy for the deacon to accept the role of the presbyter and offer ministry to the congregation rather than work to enable the congregation to minister to the community. At times this had seemed the only option. My hope was that the project would help the congregation understand my diaconal role and help me to fulfil it. What I had not yet come to understand was that this was a journey. We were setting out on a voyage of discovery, with only the starting point fixed. At this point I felt clear that diaconal ministry was a 'ministry without', in John McCarthy's words, and different from that of the presbyteral minister who ministers to the church. The deacon ministers for the church.

If my view was valid, who was there to minister to Airedale and Townville in a presbyteral way.

Chapter Three

Designing Our Project

The team decided that the purpose of our project should be twofold. Our first aim was to try to establish a clear role for a deacon which would offer the congregations a vision of diaconal ministry that would be acceptable to them, and which would be transferable to other situations. The second part of the project would be to try to return to the circuit's original objective in appointing a deacon, i.e. to help the congregations with their work in the community.

The Church as Society

If the church has a role in the local community, then what exactly is it? The team was very sure that there was a role to fulfil, but not so sure as to what it was. Some members of the team remembered the intention behind the appointment of the first deacon, but some knew nothing of this history.

One of the difficulties was the social setting in which this was taking place. While this was not a middle-class church offering charitable aid to the poor of the village, to some extent that was the model on which the deacon's appointment had been based. The original circuit decision to appoint a deacon to work in Airedale had been based on the understanding that Airedale was the most deprived area within the circuit. The Airedale church was part of that area and shared its problems. The deacon was sent to work with the congregation in the community rather than being sent from a situation of comparative affluence to aid the local situation.

A more serious difficulty was the way the Methodist Church generally has become more and more dependent upon the presbyteral minister. Both of the churches involved in this project were founded by, and originally administered by, groups of lay people. Today the congregations look to the presbyteral minister for any initiative and have vested him/her with authority and responsibility.

The Welfare state and the dependence upon authorities to deal with and solve our problems have affected the way people within the church react to life.[1] Added to this, the greater pastoral needs of ageing congregations lead to a growing dependence on the ordained ministry.

In society generally, the trend has been to use community development workers as catalysts to empower the people to act for themselves. This is a process encouraged in regeneration areas where it is usually referred to as 'capacity building'.

The circuit's intention had been that the deacon should work in this way, enabling the people to develop their own ministry to the community. The reality had been that the deacon had become the sole doer. Part of this difficulty was that the congregation had become used to the presbyteral role of ministry, where they were ministered to. Presented with a deacon as their minister, they tended to expect the same ministry. This is evidenced by some of the responses received from one of the questionnaires that we gave out to the congregations at the start of the project:

> 'The deacon spends too much time in the community and does not give sufficient time to the congregation's needs.'
> 'I think that he should spend two thirds of his time in the church and one third in the community.'

From the time that the deacon was given pastoral charge of the two churches this tension was probably inevitable.

It seemed to me that nearly six years on from the original appointment the perceptions of congregations, circuit and deacon had moved away from the original intention. The deacon was viewed now as simply a replacement presbyter and moving back to the original understanding would no longer be possible. The practical situation of the deacon could not be returned to a role alongside a minister, as the congregations involved would see this as a loss of ministry. Too many expectations had changed. A fresh start would be needed.

Devising an Action Plan

If the original aim in appointing a deacon to the work on the estates served by the churches at Airedale and Townville was to be fulfilled, we would have to create a change in understanding amongst the congregation.

The team's first requirement was that everyone should be involved and that an understanding of the deacon's role should be made available to the whole congregation. Before we could do this, it was essential to have for ourselves a clear understanding of what that role was.

I undertook the historical and biblical research of the deacon's ministry to give our thinking a context and a wider overview of how the office originated. The historical research would not be confined to the Methodist Church as the diaconate had roots far beyond that. The Methodist Diaconal Order today is engaged in talks with deacons of several other denominations in an attempt to discover a mutuality of role across the denominations. There are diaconal ministries in most of the present day denominations, and many of these are, or are moving towards, a permanent diaconate.

It was also necessary to look at the wavering development of diaconal ministries wherever they were to be found. At the same time an in-depth examination of the history of the Wesley Deaconess Order and its parallel Orders in the Primitive Methodist Church and the United Methodist Church was to be undertaken. This was to include the amalgamation of the three Orders into the Wesley Deaconess Order in 1933 and the subsequent fortunes of that Order up to its latest re-formation as the Methodist Diaconal Order in 1987.

Alongside this investigation was a consideration of the use of the word *diakonia* and its application in the foundation and formation of the modern Orders. There is reason to ask whether this word has developed a new connotation that takes it away from simply a description of the ministry of the deacon.[2]

Both *diakonia* and *diakonos,* as ecclesiological language, have their roots in the use made of them in the New Testament. My research included an examination of what these words meant to the founding fathers of the church when they began to use them in the context of ministry.

The other team members set out to find out what those who had instigated the diaconal appointment in the circuit had intended the role of the deacon to be. They were also to endeavour to discover what the understanding of other circuit officers had been in 1987/88 when the appointment was first discussed and what the understanding of the various circuit officers was today. They decided to do this through a study of the circuit documents, a series of meetings with the circuit officers, and by setting up a circuit discussion group consisting of past and present officers at circuit and church level.

Through sharing together what we learned, and informing the congregation of our findings, we hoped to be able to find a framework in which the deacon could work with integrity.

Involving the Congregations

To achieve the second change we would need to help the congregations to understand their own diaconal ministry and offer them opportunities to fulfil it.

One of the problems that had been highlighted was the lack of information that the congregation had about what the deacon was supposed to do and what he, in fact, did do. Something needed to be done about the communication gap if we were going to make any impression on the congregation as a whole. Amongst the strategies we adopted was a series of sermons that I was to preach over a three-month period. This was intended not only to inform, but to widen the area of response to the whole circuit, since the matter was of concern to the whole circuit.

A series of displays from some of the groups supported by the deacon would be created and displayed. These would be used in Townville and Airedale and then taken to other churches in the circuit. The displays would also be used in conjunction with talks I would give to Fellowship groups at churches throughout the circuit.

The third angle of approach to this problem was to involve the congregations more fully in the work that the deacon was doing in their name. This would be done through inviting speakers from a number of organisations with which the deacon was connected, or was directly involved. Among those chosen was Homestart; an organisation that works with families with children under five (I had been a member of the management committee there for three years when the project started). Then there was The Chrysalis Youth Project. This was the community project that took up more of my time than any other. I was the chairman of the steering committee that set the present project in motion and, at the time of writing, I was both Company Secretary and a Director of this project. One of the directors of Chrysalis, Lister Baynes, agreed to give a talk to the fellowship meeting which would supplement the display already in use. Lastly, there would be two speakers from the Airedale Interactive Meeting, which is an interagency grouping of people involved in working with drug users, or those affected by drug use. I had been involved with the group for four years and it met on the Airedale Methodist Church premises. The two speakers would be the community worker from the group, and the Coordinator of Gasped, a self help group for the parents of drug users.

There were two principal aims in providing this amount of information and teaching. The first was to raise awareness amongst the congregation of the work the deacon was involved in. The second was to offer an opportunity for them to take up some form of involvement in the community work themselves.

The Community Influences

The team found it useful to hear about the various community groups with which I was working. Gaining an understanding of the work already being undertaken gave them a perspective to help in deciding how to appraise the needs of the community, and where the church might be able to offer some help.

My involvement with Homestart was largely committee work and supporting the organizer, but I was able to offer specialized help with administrative organisation and assessment systems (some of the skills I brought with me from my secular life). Alongside this was the contact I made with young families through baptismal visits and referred pastoral visits, which offered opportunities to refer families for Homestart support. Occasionally these two involvements enabled me to offer a greater variety of help to these families. On some occasions the volunteers and management team found useful the counselling and pastoral skills I was able to bring into their situation.

Airedale Interactive Meeting was an interagency group through which I related to almost all the statutory and voluntary agencies on the estate. The agency personnel changed around often and so I was able to offer a degree of continuity to the group. A great deal of the focus of this group was on drugs abuse and the problems this brought to the community.

The largest commitment was my involvement with 'The Chrysalis Youth Project Limited' (see page 6). Since the inception of the project it has been managed by and funded through the church that has always sought to involve the community in the management committee. The development of the project was in its third year and the limited company had been in existence for one year. Chrysalis is a registered charity and its aims involve youth work and training. The establishment of the facility and staffing costs would be in the region of £530,000 in the first year. As Company Secretary and primary contact for all the funding bodies to whom the Chrysalis applied, I had a very large involvement in the project[3]. As we discussed this it became clear that no one on the team had any real knowledge of the magnitude of this enterprise and certainly none of the congregation was really aware of the proportion of my time taken up by it.

The Present Role Assessed

Before we could begin to work with a satisfactory understanding of my role, it was apparent that the whole team would need to be clear what my present work was. With this knowledge it would be possible to assess what was in fact the appropriate work of the deacon and to what extent it was well executed.

As a starting point it was decided to look carefully at what I was doing and how much time I gave to each part of the work with which I was involved. I agreed to keep a detailed log of my work and personal time use over a three-week period during January 1997. These were presented to the team as a series of tables with twenty-three different categories for working time and seven categories for personal time. The entire team found these charts interesting reading. Much to my surprise there was a general lack of awareness as to the amount of time involved in service preparation. When the time for delivering and preparing for all the services in a week was added together, it totalled twenty-nine per cent of the total sixty-four hours used for working during a week.[4] Most of the team, but particularly those currently in employment felt that an average working week of sixty-four hours was unreasonable and could be detrimental to the health of the deacon. Since my own background includes production management and time and motion study experience, I could only agree. There is a considerable body of evidence to indicate that excessive hours of work lead to a drop in actual productivity and it would seem reasonable that this should apply to ministry also. Those who have investigated overwork amongst the clergy[5] have come to the conclusion that tired ministers lead to tired ministry. The team felt that it was important that this should receive some attention during the project.

At the same time the team had three meetings at which to make their own assessment of the work that the deacon might be expected to do. These meetings were organized by Janette Woodhead who acted as facilitator and helped them to produce a response which could be used as some form of measure. They produced two lists. First a list of 'Things you want done by the deacon', later described by one of the team as a 'wish list'. There were thirty-eight items on this list covering a very wide range of tasks and skills, but they in fact broke down into two groups, although this was not immediately obvious. The first group consisted of all the things that a presbyteral minister would do within the church, what could be described as practical tasks, i.e.; weddings, funerals, baptisms, conduct of worship, and pastoral visiting. The second group was more general: within this group were terms such as, 'mediator', 'confidant', 'advocate' and 'representative for change'.

The second list contained their estimates of how the deacon spent his time. This list actually reflected a good knowledge, within the team, of some of the ways that my time is used in the church. There was some resistance however to identifying times. No one was prepared to offer times for service preparation, study, or outreach work. This was to prove unhelpful in making comparisons between the two sets of charts. There seemed to be an awareness in the team that these three items would involve a considerable amount of time and, if included in the calculations, would show an expectation of working time much greater than they were prepared to own.

Evaluation Procedures

The principal evaluation procedure agreed on by the team was that of questionnaires. To provide a starting point for the assessment procedure it was decided to give all members of the congregations a questionnaire to complete before the project was started. This would give us a baseline of congregational understanding of diaconal ministry from which we would be able to assess what changes had taken place in people's thinking after the project had been completed. This survey would be looked at again at the end of the project and compared with the results of a questionnaire to be created in light of the project.

Ministerial Development Possibilities

The primary need was to establish what the ministry of a deacon is. This would involve a wide-ranging examination of the subject which would be capable of offering a definition acceptable to the Methodist Church as a whole. It was also important that these findings should not be at variance with the traditions of the wider church in any significant way. Alongside the need for a valid description, was the important task of rediscovering what were the local church's, and the circuit's, expectations of a deacon

During the project it was hoped that the development of the community contacts already in place, and the creation of a wider community base would provide opportunities to develop the deacon's skills in this facet of diaconal ministry. Community involvement was part of the job description of the deacon in the circuit and was also part of the expectation of the MDO.

There was a realisation within the team that there was a lack of confidence in diaconal ministry as a response to the needs of the congregation. This had tended to create a situation in which the deacon's self confidence had been eroded. It was felt that the church and the deacon would be helped in making constructive changes if we could engender more conviction in the congregation that diaconal ministry was appropriate to the needs of the church in the area.

The team felt that providing clear definitions and descriptions would help a deacon to have faith that the congregation understood and supported what was being done , and this would allow him or her to develop his/her ministry.

Chapter Four

The Project - Working Together

Introduction

The project took place during the first half of 1998. The work done in the previous year had established the problem, which we had defined in the following statement: 'The Methodist congregations of Airedale and Townville, who are without a presbyteral minister, are unclear about the role of the deacon in the church and in the local community.' The goals we had set ourselves were, first, to clarify the role of the deacon in the context of the Methodist churches at Airedale and Townville, and then to enable the two congregations to recognize and develop their own ministry to the local community. The team and I had decided upon a three-pronged strategy to achieve these goals: researching the role of the deacon; researching the history of the diaconal appointment in Airedale and Townville; and sharing our findings with the congregations.[1]

Researching the Role of the Deacon

The first prong was a programme of work to be undertaken by myself[2]. The magazines of the Order[3] provided a good resource for a study of the history of the MDO and helped me to gain a real insight into the work of the Order during the twentieth century. These were read at the Order's motherhouse in Birmingham. The libraries of Queen's College Birmingham and the Urban Theology Unit in Sheffield provided sources for some lines of research. The vast resources of the Internet made possible accessing many of the older manuscripts as well as many modern papers.

The fruits of this research are contained in a full version in chapters five, six and seven but what was needed for the team meetings was a summary. The task I had been asked to do was not to find out about deacons and their ministry, but to explain it to the team in its historical and Methodist contexts. I produced a summary of the reading and thinking which I had been able to do, which was given to each of the team and then discussed over several further meetings

The Material for Discussion

Our meetings started with some explanation of the summary they had been given and then moved into a discussion under a series of headings that I had suggested. The structure was loose and the summary was referred to often.

The material we used for these meetings was first presented as a whole. It was then broken down under the headings 'Models' and 'Images' for more detailed discussion. We started by reading Matt 20.20–28. In this passage Paulos Mar Gregorios identifies what he calls: 'The four necessary conditions of an authentic Diakonia.'

i) the willingness to suffer with those whom one serves and to give of oneself

ii) humility as opposed to superiority about oneself, and respect as opposed to condescension towards those to be served

iii) not using *Diakonia* as an occasion for domination, privilege and rank

iv) willingness to identify with the served to the point of laying down one's life for their sake.[4]

If Christ is our model for authentic *diakonia,* it cannot be a *diakonia* which involves no cost to us other than the use of our money or our 'personnel' (those we employ to represent us).

We also considered Luke 22.27 of which Gerard Hughes says:

'We can escape the demands of this teaching by seeing it as applying only to church officials. However, we are all "Christs", all called to serve rather than be served.'[5]

In this passage Luke uses the term *diakoneo,* which would seem to be a statement about the kind of service that Jesus is suggesting, as lowly service rather than the 'ministry' of high office.

The second half of the first meeting was devoted to considering the term 'deacon' in the New Testament writings, other than the gospels, trying to come to an understanding of how it had been used and at what point it came to be seen as an office rather than a function.

In the second, and subsequent meetings, I explained something of the writings of the Church Fathers and the history of diaconal ministry up to the present day. This led us to a close examination of the growth of diaconal ministries in the later nineteenth and early twentieth centuries when a number of new forms of diaconal ministry sprang up throughout Europe.[6]

All of these new forms of diaconal work were instituted in response to a perceived need for the Church to respond to the community that it claimed to serve. Each of the diaconal patterns offered charitable service to the community in its own way. Nursing care of the poor was one particular form it took.

What all of these new diaconates had in common was a view of diaconal ministry that was based on two differing traditions. The first tradition had its origins with the seven chosen for table service in Acts 6. Despite the fact that modern scholarship casts doubts on this understanding of the seven, they have been seen as deacons from the earliest times[7]. The Church has also used the description of their setting apart as the foundation for its thinking about diaconal ministry.

The second drew on the tradition of the 'suffering servant' and the theology of Christ the Servant as exemplified in the gospels (Matt 20, Luke 22 and others). Embodying this servanthood was believed to have been the purpose of the deacon in ancient times and was reinforced by the descriptions of deacons in the writings of the early Church fathers.[8]

Whether or not we could establish that such an understanding of the origins of the deacon's ministry was poorly founded seems to me to be irrelevant to the process through which the diaconal orders were founded. The starting point for these new diaconates was a tradition which had been within the Church since the end of the first century AD; that the deacon was the focus of the Church's charity, and that diaconal ministry should represent Christ as servant, in distinction to priest or shepherd.

The tradition of the deacon within British Methodism, and the United Methodist Church in America is now more than a hundred years old. The Lutheran tradition is nearly 150 years old. Within the Roman Catholic Church the revival of the permanent diaconate springs from the early 1950s, but is seen as an unbroken link with the past. In all of these traditions, as in others such as the Church of Scotland, the United Church in Canada and the Uniting Church in Australia, the statements they make on the calling and function are about charity and enabling. The deacon's place within the liturgy varies from the high profile place, as described in the Roman Catholic papers from Vatican II onwards, through the wide opportunities in the United Methodist understanding, as stated in their 1996 book of discipline, to the Swedish Lutheran deacon who has no liturgical function at all.[9] In the ordination service for deacons the Methodist Church in Britain offers a description of what it means to represent Christ the servant, but has not yet offered any guidance on a liturgical role.

The place of the deacon in the early Church is unclear. Even in the second and third centuries we have little information on which to base any idea of their function in the Church of the day. Despite this, the tradition of a servant ministry of charity, proclamation, and contact with the sick and the needy persisted. It would be difficult, however, to show what form this took or to provide recorded instances which would illustrate the tradition of servant ministry as the origins of the tradition are lost to history, as are the records of early diaconal ministry.

What is important is that the Churches have kept the tradition of the diaconate alive and have reawakened it in recent years. The upsurge in interest has been driven by renewed awareness that the service we owe to God is a two-sided coin consisting of *leitourgia* (worship) and *diakonia* (service to others in Christ's name). Perhaps the best description I have encountered for the ministry of the deacon comes from the United Methodist Church. 'It is the deacons, in both persona and function, whose distinctive ministry is to embody, articulate, and lead the whole people of God in its servant ministry.'[10]

Models of Deacon

As the meetings progressed we could see a number of models for the office of deacon emerging from our discussion of this material. All of these had been valid at some time and some of them are in use today in one denomination or another. We looked at each of the models we discerned and tried to evaluate them within the context of the Methodist Church and the Castleford Circuit in particular.

Models in the Gospels

It very soon became clear to us that there was no model for the deacon in the Gospels. Gregorios' description of Christ as the model for authentic *diakonia* points to characteristics that are theological parameters[11] that would define the perfect deacon. The team felt that these were not helpful parameters by which to measure a human deacon; in particular they had problems with the fourth of Gregorios' statements[12]. One member asked me sceptically: 'Does it mean that you would be willing to lay down your life for someone?' He added that it was a nonsense to assume that of anyone.

What became clear was that the terms *diakoneo, diakonia* and *diakonos,* as used in the Gospels could be reference points for modelling, but what the team felt was most important was the context from which *they* were approaching this situation, i.e. a deacon in pastoral care of their churches.

Models from the New Testament Epistles and the Early Church

Within the New Testament writings there was insufficient hard information to build a diaconal model that we could use. The points of interest were the ideas that emerged from discussion of Paul's use of deacon in the light of Collins's interpretation of the term as meaning someone who is sent.[12] This fitted easily with the perception we all had of a deacon as a minister under discipline, going wherever he or she might be sent rather than seeking invitation to a place of choice.[13] What troubled the team was the model, presented by the early church, of an assistant to the bishop, acting as a go-between for the bishop from one side and for the congregation from the other. Such a model does not sit easily with a Methodist congregation. The team rejected the presbyter substituting for the bishop in that relationship on the grounds that it would seem to elevate the presbyter in a way that the team found inappropriate.

The representative aspect inherent in that model was much less clearly understood and had to be teased out more carefully. It was when we went on to ask the question 'Who sent the deacon?' that we began to see some comparisons with modern practice. The deacon may have been 'sent' by the bishop in the early church, but in the present situation there is much more likely to be a variety of 'senders'. In the Airedale and Townville context we felt that there were two such 'senders'. Establishing who was the sender, and therefore whom the deacon represented, caused us to explore a number of options.

We had started by assuming that the sender was the Methodist church, but came to see that the authority that a deacon possesses comes from his/her relationship with the Order. So we came to the conclusion that the Order was our first 'sender' as the deacons had been sent to the circuit by the Order.

We concluded that the second 'sender' was the local circuit. I had started the process with the idea that it was the local congregation whom I represented. Our early discussions and the first statements we worked with assumed that the congregation was the immediate 'sender'. What our discussions and our researches showed was that the authority was vested in the circuit meeting. It was at circuit level that decisions about the work of the deacon were taken and therefore it could only be with its authority that the deacon was vested.

Lutheran and Wesleyan models

Because Thomas Bowman Stephenson, the founder of the Wesley Deaconess Order, visited the Lutheran Deaconess houses and studied their work, the Lutheran model could be presented as the inspiration for the Wesley Deaconess Order, but there were major differences. From very early in its history the Deaconess Order was owned by the church at an institutional level. Almost from the beginning the Wesley deaconesses had been involved in mission and therefore in teaching the gospel faith. This church-centredness had not been evident in the Lutheran Orders that were not owned in an institutional way by the Lutheran Church. The Lutheran deaconesses principally lived in community and paralleled other religious orders in their structures. The Wesley Deaconess Order was a dispersed community with a motherhouse. From the very early days the Methodist Church took the Order under its authority.

That the members of the Order should be visibly part of the church and that the church should own their work, either centrally or locally, was discussed at this meeting. There were those in the team who did not see any great necessity to identify the charitable works of the deacon with the church. Some felt that people in the wider community might be more ready to accept what was offered if it was offered without any apparent church connection.

When we came to consider the Wesley Deaconess Order as our model, we found that there were differences between the situation of their day and ours. Until its 'refoundation'[16] as the Methodist Diaconal Order, the stipend for deaconesses had always been quite considerably lower than that for presbyteral ministers. The working conditions and other patterns of employment had been different also. Despite the fact that the church had decided, in 1966, that it was possible for a deaconess to marry and still remain in the Order, the complications had never been taken into account in any practical way. So, for example, a married deaconess could not be stationed in the normal way because there was no provision for suitable accommodation, neither was her stipend sufficient to support a family. There were, and seem always to have been, presumptions about the acceptance of this sort of situation. David Mullan, writing of the New Zealand Order, has said:

> 'Until recent years, when the two orders began to merge their education and deployment characteristics, the Order had witnessed to the genuine nature of *diakonia* or caring service. It rarely displayed an 'up front' image. This was partly because regulations denied deaconesses the right to 'ministerial' seats in Conference, though they were allowed two to 'represent' the Order. They were, somehow, neither ministerial nor 'lay'. And it was more significantly due to their own estimate of themselves: their understanding of their 'status' led them to the kind of humility that characterises the true servant.'

It was in their nature.[17]

This sort of understanding has also been part of the view of the Order in Britain. Such a statement could have been made within the Methodist Church of Great Britain for many of the same reasons. The belief that 'it was in their nature' and that those who entered the Deaconess Orders were possessed of a nature so humble that they desired nothing more in life than to serve in the shadows cast by the less humble, seems to be based largely on a desire that there should be such people, rather than on the reality of their existence. In *Diakonia and the Moa,* Mullan tells us that when presbyteral ministry was opened to women, in the New Zealand context, there was a sharp fall in the recruitment to the Order. Then when the Order was opened to men, all but one of the remaining active deaconesses offered for presbyteral ministry. In Britain, when presbyteral ministry was opened to women, a great many of the active deaconesses offered for it, and recruitment to the Wesley Deaconess Order came to such a low ebb that the Order was closed to recruitment for ten years. Although this self-effacing humble deaconess model had existed for many years, it was clearly not authentic.

There was no wish in the team to see this sort of model used for diaconal ministry today. There was great admiration for the role played by the deaconesses in the mission halls and in the Home Mission caravans, but that was not applicable to their own immediate context.

A Roman Catholic Model

The last model considered was that presented by the non-stipendiary deacons in the Roman Catholic Church and in some of the Lutheran churches in America. There have been developments of this kind in presbyteral ministry within Methodism. Ministers in Local Appointment were authorized in 1988 and have increased in number since that time. MLA's, as they are usually called, are not itinerant, which means that they are not available for stationing by Conference[18]. They are stationed in their home circuit, or some neighbouring circuit where a suitable appointment has been set up. They minister to a church, or churches, by agreement, but continue in secular employment thus not normally being available for pastoral concerns during their usual working hours. We did not consider MLA to be a suitable model for the deacon since Methodist deacons are members of a religious order and a willingness to 'be sent' is a sign of their being under discipline.

Roman Catholic deacons are members of the church clergy who live and work in the community. They carry out their liturgical functions at the normal services on Sunday, and during the week they carry out a representative role in some areas of church life.[19] Although Roman Catholic deacons are clearly understood to be clerics, they have something in common with Methodist local preachers, since the Methodist church originally differentiated local preachers from ordained presbyters by the minister's calling to work within the church full time and itinerate.

Although I had found much of value in the Roman
Catholic concept of 'deacon' the team did not find it very
helpful as a role model for our purposes.

Images the Team found Useful

The team looked at the various images of diaconal
ministry uncovered by the research. Images were words or
ideas that created a picture in our minds which might, or
might not, help us to understand the deacon's role more
clearly.

An Enabler

Deacons are often called 'enablers'. The suggestion made
is that their task is to enable the ministry of others.
Considerable discussion took place amongst the team around
this concept. The idea that the deacon should enable others
to fulfil their ministry was accepted in a very positive light,
but there was some lack of clarity about what was meant by
'their ministry'. The team agreed that they themselves had
Christian duties and most saw themselves as having a role in
the church, but no one really saw these duties as their
'ministry' and even less as their calling. To some extent this is
a question of language and in that respect would not have a
great deal of relevance to the problem in its essence. Much
more importantly, there is an underlying sense in which some
understand their place in the church as the 'ministered to'.
Despite the obvious works they may do within the church,
they do not feel that they are a part of the ministry of the
church, more that they are part of the congregation who are
supporting the church.

Although the team's discussions on this image were
positive about the principle, there was a definite resistance to
the end purpose of such a principle. The team were
comfortable with the idea of 'enabling' as a style of ministry,
but what should be enabled was less clear.

A Go-between

The image of go-between was one with which they were comfortable.[20] The team were quite content that I should act as go-between for themselves, as congregation, and the wider community. I was less happy with this image. In the early church the deacon acted as a buffer zone, so that the congregation should not take up the bishop's time unless it was necessary to do so. That was how the go-between had worked and I did not think that was a particularly suitable image for the deacon when used vis-à-vis the congregation's relationship with the community.

An Ambassador

Another image looked at by Collins was that of ambassador[21]. It could be thought to have many similarities to the go-between, but it has quite distinct connotations that we found more interesting and helpful. An ambassador acts with authority because he or she is deemed to represent the sending authority in a substitutionary way. In this way ambassadors act as though they were in fact the person whom they represent. In this sense a deacon should act and be seen by the wider community as the congregation/circuit by whom he or she was sent. This tends to mean that the church is seen to be present in the community when the deacon is present on its behalf. An essential corollary to this image is that the deacon has to have visible presence. This is, at present, less easy for a Methodist deacon than it is for an Anglican or Roman Catholic. The deaconesses in the past had a quite distinct uniform that marked them out. The uniform prescribed for the present-day deacon, male or female, is indistinguishable from normal dress.

It is even more difficult for the deacon to be an ambassador for the community in the church and in making that role clearly visible.[22] Some deacons seem to attempt this through dress. Since most diaconal stations are in disadvantaged areas, it is not uncommon to see deacons who have adopted the style of the community in which they work, appearing at services or church functions in the casual everyday clothing of the young people in the community.

Whether it is a distinctive uniform which indicates the church's presence, or a distinctive style to show that the community is represented in the church, it is hard to see how both purposes can be served by one dress style. Writing about the rush of presbyters to abandon the clerical collar in the 1960s Mullan says:

'Most who were uncomfortable in the collar twenty years ago were also uncomfortable doing many things that the church required of them. They were more enthusiastic about getting 'out of the church' into the wider world, to serve the community without the trappings of the church *and its beliefs.*

But this question arises, to what were they motivated? Were they in fact as clearly motivated to the service of the church-in-the-congregation as they were to the church-in-the-community? If the latter, one might argue that their primary motivation was actually diaconal rather than presbyteral. If such were the case *then their unwillingness to be identified as 'religious' can be seen to be reasonable.*[24]'

Both in the imagery of the ambassador and of 'the representative', which we will look at next, the idea of the deacon hiding his/her identity and working in the community incognito, is not a possibility.

The Representative (or Exemplary Imagery)

This image proved difficult for the team in that, when applied to ministry, 'representative' means to provide an image of. When offered this interpretation the team were unsure of whom, or what, the deacon should provide a representation. They were very uncomfortable with the suggestion that this should be of Christ the servant. The possibility of representing Christ, even partially, seemed unacceptable to them.

Most of the team found the modern usage of 'the representative' in the sense of 'the company representative' quite acceptable. They could see the role in terms of the ambassador image, being sent on behalf of.

This response to the classic use of representative as applied to ministry was revealing, and to some extent disturbing. Throughout this book I have applied the term in this way to convey the idea of representational ministry. If the team's response to this usage were to be shown as a widespread one, it would suggest that this theological understanding of ministry might not be shared with the whole church.

A Focus

The last image to come out of the research was that of a focus. The team were happy to accept the deacon as a focus for the charitable work of the church and for the work of the church in the community; where the deacon is, the work of the church can be seen clearly and sharply. Photographers and painters draw the viewer in to the main subject in this way. In a good photograph the eye is drawn unerringly to the point of focus, and it was in this way that the deacon was seen to be a focus for the work of the church in the community.

A Doorkeeper

Finally we looked at an image much used by those within the Methodist Church and occasionally others, that of the doorkeeper. It is usually suggested that the doorkeeper has a foot both inside and outside the threshold of the church, but this was not how the team understood the image. The door steward in Methodism is the greeter, but has no role in reaching out and, unfortunately, seems to have little in the way of recognition within the congregation. The team required a more pro-active role for the deacon. They were willing for the deacon to demonstrate a measure of humility, but not to be a humble doorman and for them the doorkeeper was not a helpful image.

Researching the History of the Diaconal Appointment in Airedale and Townville

This second prong of our project was led by Peter Wadsworth who was one of the circuit stewards in office during the period when the first deacon was in the circuit, and who had seen some of the changes in the appointment. He was asked by the team to set up a circuit discussion group consisting of some of the present circuit officers and those who had been in office at the time the first deacon's appointment was sought. With the aid of Maureen Dean, another team member and a present circuit steward, he arranged a series of meetings with them. The purpose was to ascertain what they understood about the decisions taken in 1989 and then to determine whether the appointment had gone as they expected.

Alongside this work the team were looking at the original papers concerning the appointment and the application for a deacon (deaconess at the time[24]). What emerged was a catalogue of confusion. Many of the remembered decisions and situations do not match the written records. Worryingly, some of the most persistent differences uncovered were of generally held views that had created feelings of unhappiness in those who held these memories. The most important of these concerned the area of work of the diaconal appointment and how the original deaconess would relate to the circuit.

The letter of application for a deaconess to be appointed to the Castleford circuit is ambiguous in this matter. With hindsight, it is possible to see that the writer had the intention that the deaconess should concentrate in a particular geographical area:

'With the present ministerial staff of two the work involved would lay too great a demand upon them, and the Circuit Meeting, therefore, decided to ask for a deacon or deaconess to increase the leadership potential in the Circuit, *and also to work in a specific area.*'

'The work of the deaconess would be predominantly in the most 'deprived' area of the circuit served by two churches, establishing the work of those churches to serve the needs of the community in conjunction with the Social Services and other agencies. *She would also help in the Circuit life* especially with training for work with young people[25].'
It is equally possible to interpret the references to circuit to mean that the deaconess would have a much wider role and this, it seems, is how it was remembered by some of those involved.

One of the concerns uppermost in the mind of the circuit ministers when making this application was the situation at Airedale. As far back as the circuit reports of 1965 there had been concerns about this church, and the 1972 report paints a particularly bleak picture:
'This has been the first year that the circuit has been run by three ministers - the smallest number of Methodist ministers in the area for over a century . . .

. . . If there is to be a continuing Methodist witness in that area (Airedale), there will be need for far greater lay leadership and a concentration over a long period. It is a far from normal situation.[26]'
Although the witness of the church at Airedale had obviously continued, the concerns expressed in 1965 and 1972 were still present and, as will be noted from the 1989 letter, the circuit ministerial staff was now reduced to two.

This situation was clearly in the mind of the writer, but perhaps not everyone had the same focus.[27]

What became clear in the discussions which the team had with the circuit discussion group was that several of those involved at the time, including one circuit steward, understood that the deaconess was to work around the circuit, not only at Airedale. What they remembered about the tasks to be undertaken by the deaconess was expressed in statements such as: 'mainly work in the community', 'outreach in the name of the church' and 'social work'. All agreed that it was a circuit appointment.

What had caused the situation to change from conception to actuality? The two principal reasons were established, as the differing perceptions of the superintendent and some of the circuit stewards (largely a matter of emphasis) and the fact that the role of the deaconess had been changed to include pastoral charge of Airedale and Townville after two years in post. Some of those involved in the earlier decision had not been as involved with the later changes and that had left them with no understanding of how the situation evolved.

A Changing Role

Through their research into the papers, and the discussions with the circuit group, the team had been able to put together a picture of the diaconal appointment in the circuit and how it had changed over the nine years. As they had been personally involved with the ministry which came out of that appointment, they were now able to look at what had happened and compare it to the intention of the original statements. In making these comparisons they were able to see the effect that the changes had on the perceptions of the members of the circuit, and the members of Airedale and Townville in particular, as the circuit began to feel they were being less well served by the deacon, and Airedale and Townville took ownership of a 'minister'. The following is a summary of the circuit discussion group's findings:

The Beginnings

The request for a deacon/deaconess to be stationed in the circuit originated in 1988 and came out of what was an increasingly desperate situation. There was a serious difficulty in maintaining the work of the circuit, with the two ministers feeling stretched beyond hope of improving the situation by their own efforts. For more than ten years the ministerial staff had struggled, their only hope being for a more active and involved lay leadership to improve things. In particular it was growing steadily more difficult to maintain the work at Airedale.

The demography of the circuit did not help. Airedale and Townville were ministered to from Kippax, at the far end of the circuit. The effectiveness of this depended upon the drive and commitment of the minister involved, but it was never easy. As a section[28], there was no coherence. People from Kippax and Airedale could only reach each other with considerable difficulty by public transport, and not at all on a Sunday.

A Pastoral Charge

As described previously, there was a change in the deacon's appointment after 1991. This realignment of the deacon's role meant that her visible presence in the wider circuit work was diminished. The intention was that the circuit would gain more of the time and energy of the presbyteral ministers. It was in the Kippax section that this gain was least well understood. When, looked at with hindsight, this is understandable. The deacon was no longer a circuit minister, but belonged to two churches in the circuit. One of the well-recognized syndromes within the church is the impression in people's minds that 'if you can't see the minister they are not actually working at that time'. What the Kippax section had gained was more of their presbyteral minister's time and energy. This was very difficult to quantify, and perceivable only with effort. What they had lost was obvious and they were quick to notice the deacon's absence from the work she had previously done in their churches.

Community Work

One of the understandings held by those responsible for the first appointment was that the deacon would work mainly in the community. By this they meant the community to which the churches related, rather than in the congregations. It does seem likely that each committee member had the community to which their own church related in mind when this was agreed. The superintendent's intention had always been that the community with which the deacon would work was that in Airedale.[29]

It was from Airedale that the Social Service request for help had come and it was this community which had been used as the point of need in the applications. From our conversations with past circuit officials and church stewards it was clear that they had not all understood what this meant. Their lack of a clear understanding of the focus of the appointment was added to during the first two years when the deacon's work took her into the wider circuit. After the change there was a growing feeling that they had lost the deacon.

More importantly, the 1991 changes meant that the deacon's work had taken on a much larger element of congregational pastoral care than had been the original intention. This could not fail to affect the time given to the community work. There had been a shift in emphasis.

Community involvement continued, but it could no longer occupy the time that had been intended at the start. Much good work was being done, but for the largest part of the congregation the ministerial image was presbyteral. This image hardened and grew more focused over the next three years. Glenda, the deacon, came more and more to fulfil the role of the presbyteral minister for the congregation at Airedale, and gradually this affected her own understanding of her sense of ministry. One of the consequences of this change was the change in her view of her calling mentioned on page ?. Moving the focus had changed what people saw and the changes affected everyone. The Circuit, the congregation and Glenda had all radically changed.

The consequence for Glenda and the circuit was that she had to be freed from her appointment. In 1994 the Circuit wrote an application for a renewed diaconal appointment to start from September 1994. In this much shorter application there was still a primary place given to community work, but the outline of the appointment was quite different.

'The broad 'profile' is that of developing the links created between the church and the community. For this the a
Appointment requires pastoral care of the church families, and a willingness to conduct baptisms, weddings and funerals through which many contacts are made with people 'outside the church'. The appointment needs a continuing relationship with the social services centres in the community[30].'

A New Appointment

This was the appointment to which I was stationed in 1994. The background was unknown to me and I had only the application form as guidance. While not ideal, there seemed no reason why this should not be an acceptable diaconal appointment.

The discussions with the circuit group and the team clarified some of the areas of difficulty that had created the problem, which the project was seeking to examine. Many within the circuit had expected that the new deacon would become a circuit resource, as had been the hope for the original appointment. They had failed to grasp that the circuit had made changes in that early role. The congregation expected a replacement for the 'deacon in a presbyteral image' which they had lost. The language used, by those responsible for briefing the deacon on his new responsibilities was all about community. As a deacon I had my own perceptions.

What became clear in these discussions with the circuit group was that neither the circuit, the congregations at Airedale and Townville, nor I myself, had our needs met, as we would have wanted. The circuit had not seen any more of the deacon than had been the case previously. In fact, since I had not undertaken the work of circuit trainer, they actually saw less. The congregations were grieving over their loss of a 'minister' and were angry with the church because Glenda had not been successful in her candidature. I came to realize that what they had wanted was that I should pick up the presbyteral role where Glenda had been forced to put it down. Many in the congregation were highly supportive of what they perceived as my loss in not being able to preside at Holy Communion. This was not something that I desired, but they seemed unable to understand that.

I was striving to fulfil the role of a deacon as written, and as described by the superintendent (see page 24). The community emphasis was where I put my focus. Even in the liturgical roles of baptisms, weddings and funerals these came mostly from community contacts.   In particular there were many baptisms. Since I understood that these were to be used to reach into the community I embraced them enthusiastically.   A   baptism   visit   gave   a   tremendous opportunity to teach people outside the church about the gospel in a way that was almost impossible elsewhere. This emphasis was less popular with the congregation, many of whom felt that these people were 'using the church'. Each group was pulling in a different direction, all wondering why expectations were not being met.

Sharing Our Findings with the Congregation

This third strategic prong ran very much in parallel with the other two. Our purpose was to enable the congregation to recognize diaconal ministry as a ministry for all, not vested solely in the deacon. I have headed it a teaching programme because the congregations had a great deal to learn about what the deacon did on their behalf, the people with whom he worked, and the reasons for so doing.

One of the early discoveries from the team's discussions about the deacon's work was that it was not widely known. They had highlighted a communications problem that had to be overcome. Given the bare information about what the deacon actually did, it had been decided that biblical reflection on the idea of diaconal ministry would help the congregations at Townville and Airedale to accept responsibility for the ministry done in their name, and perhaps become more actively involved in it themselves.

The congregations would be most accessible during Sunday worship. This prompted the strategy of the series of sermons. There were to be three sermons, each of which would be given at both churches. In the event, the sermons were also delivered to other churches in the circuit as our sense of the ownership of the ministry of the deacon by the circuit grew.

At Airedale there are regular, well-attended fellowship meetings which were to be offered speakers from the various agencies with which I was involved. It was hoped that this would give an insight into the areas of work in which the deacon was involved as their deacon, and therefore in which they were involved as those who sent me. Most of the speakers would not include a biblical or theological input in their talks, but I followed the series with a talk that would help to focus their information theologically.

It had seemed a good idea to offer a series of bible studies as a means of reflection on diaconal ministry, but bible study groups had often been poorly attended. Since the period of the project included Lent, there would have been competition with the Lent bible studies which are much better attended. With agreement from all the churches involved (the Lent group is ecumenical), I offered a series of bible studies for Lent on the theme of the servant ministry. The ecumenical nature of these groups brought a new dimension to the discussion.

The agencies that were able to provide the exhibitions we had planned to coincide with these events were Homestart, the Chrysalis Youth Project, and AIM.

The Sermons

The first of these was delivered at Airedale in February and at Townville and Kippax in March. Entitled 'What is a deacon for', the theme explored was on the variety of gifts, concentrating on how these gifts are exercised in the ordained ministries, and the representative role of the two forms of ordained ministry. It was the representative role of the deacon's office that I hoped to explain.

The second in the series of sermons was entitled 'Christ the Servant'. It was in this service that the Homestart display was present in church and I invited the congregation to consider whether there was a way in which they could serve through Homestart. I endeavoured to show the relationship between the servant ministry as suggested in the Gospel sayings of Jesus and the examples he offered, the church's ministry as the body of Christ, and the role of the deacon as the agent of the church.

The third of these sermons was delivered at a morning service at Airedale Church and in the evening at Trinity, the largest church in the circuit. The title was 'A Ministry for All', based on the sayings of Jesus in Matthew 20:28 ('the Son of Man did not come to be served but to serve') and Matthew 25:45 ('Truly, I say to you, as you did it not to one of the least of these, you did it not to me'). It was through this particular sermon that I hoped to make the point that diaconal ministry was not the prerogative of the deacon, but was the responsibility of every Christian.

I introduced this sermon with a quotation from the statement from the United Methodist Church in America on 'The Deacon's Ministry', 'It is the deacons, in both persona and function, whose distinctive ministry it is to embody, articulate, and lead *the whole people of God in its servant ministry*'. In this description persona comes before function and I used this to differentiate between diaconal ministry and the ministry of the deacon. I tried to express this as follows:

'But it is not the DOING that is important, it is the BEING. I can do things invisibly. I can do things quietly. I could even do things somewhere else. All of these could be my own servant ministry, but they would not be the ministry of the deacon. . . .You are all servants. All have a diaconal ministry. The distinctive calling of the deacon is to make a picture with his or her BEING so that you can see more clearly how to carry this out.'

It is the deacon's characterisation of the servant which is the point of her or his ministry not the fulfilment of specific functions however good or worthwhile these functions might be.

The Speakers

The talks were given to one or other of two fellowships meeting in the church. The Tuesday Fellowship was for both men and women and had a varied pattern of activities from bible studies to slide shows. The Wednesday Fellowship was the Women's Bright Hour, which had a membership of older ladies from both the church and the wider community. Bright Hour often took the form of a simple service, but had a programme of speakers in addition.

The Probation Service

The first community project to offer a speaker was the Probation Service, who sent a representative to the Tuesday Fellowship. Irena Barnes was a probation officer who had organized help for the families of prisoners. Food and clothing were collected at the Probation Office and were distributed to those in need. For most of those who heard her talk this was a new idea. Irena opened up for them the idea that the families of offenders may also be victims, rather than society's view of them as offender. She explained her project to them and brought home to the members the effect that having the family's main provider in jail could have on the family. Some of the problems she helped her listeners to understand included the cost in time and money in visiting prisoners; she brought home to them the need of children to maintain some relationship with their father, and the effect on offenders if they lost all family contact. These extra stresses and costs could make difficult feeding and clothing the family.

Homestart

Homestart works with families with children under five years old. It is concerned with offering befriending, through trained volunteers, to young families struggling in some way. It was the second project to provide us with a speaker. Jenny Brown, co-ordinator for the Castleford and Pontefract office of Homestart, was able to interest the Ladies' Bright Hour in the work which Homestart is doing in the area and in particular on the Airedale estate. The Homestart premises are in the grounds of Redhill Junior School, not far from the church, and the deacon has represented the church on the management committee since Homestart came into being in the area. Jenny explained how Homestart operates and described the work of a volunteer for the organisation. I was able to explain to the group the work Glenda and then I did with this organisation. The ladies were interested in this work particularly as it was something they understood. Many of their questions afterwards indicated the feeling they had that there was something wrong with modern families that this sort of support had to come from outside. This led to discussion about the changes in family life and society in general during their lifetime.

The AIM Group

Keith Challen, the Drugs Action Team Coordinator for Wakefield Health Authority came to speak on behalf of AIM. I act as coordinator for this group and the church provides a meeting place. The work of the group is wide ranging and its membership includes a large number of agencies and groups, not all of whom are active within it. Keith spoke of the problems on the estate and some of the initiatives that AIM has created to alleviate them. Because AIM is not funded directly by any statutory organisation, and has no offices or facilities of its own,
arranging meetings has always been a difficulty. The contribution that the church makes to the group is twofold. First it supplies the need for premises at no cost, making it possible for the group to meet, and on two occasions providing a venue for drugs awareness courses for which the church provided the catering as well as the venue. The second contribution is the time and energy that I put into the group. In my role as coordinator I was able to offer secretarial facilities, and as enabler to see that meetings could happen in a warm and comfortable venue.

One of the problems for AIM has always been its loose structure. Although there is a wide membership, commitment tends to be low and people attend for a time and then their agency commitments mean that they cannot attend for several meetings. My role has been to offer a permanent and stable presence that was able to bring continuity to the meetings. It was gratifying to hear the approval of the Bright

Hour membership in the work, but, as usual, the questions tended to come to me at a later date.

GASPED[32]

Later in the project a speaker from one of the groups affiliated to AIM was able to come at short notice. Kristine Smith is the coordinator and founder of GASPED, a charity supporting parents with children who have drug problems. This was not a group in which church members as such could become active, but it was one which was taken very much to heart in both congregations. Kristine explained what GASPED did and how the helpline it operated was manned. She explained to the Tuesday Fellowship how I worked on the management committee for GASPED, helping particularly in doing the application work needed for GASPED to achieve charitable status. This was a difficult subject to bring to the fellowship group as much of the work done by GASPED is confidential. The group was interested in GASPED and warmed to Kristine. Although most people in the group had some awareness that drugs were a problem in the area, Kristine's personal story touched them and several of them approached and spoke with her after the talk was finished. Because of the membership's response to Kristine herself and the frankness of her personal story, there was a more immediate response than usual. Several people asked how they could help.

The Chrysalis Youth Project

The last of this group of speakers was Lister Baynes, Wakefield Metropolitan District's Principal Youth Officer, who sits on the management committee of the Chrysalis Youth Project. Lister was invited to speak to the Tuesday Fellowship about this Project, in particular to explain the latest developments within the work.

The members of the fellowship were familiar with Chrysalis in a general way as it had been part of the church's involvement for some years. The new developments, becoming a company limited by guarantee, a registered charity in its own right and working to acquire funding for a million pound training project, was new to many of them. The chairman of the fellowship had been on the original Chrysalis management committee, but had resigned when the new venture started. He had felt that this was too big a project for him and that he did not understand much of what was being discussed at the meetings about budgets, planning permissions and contracts. Despite this he was keen to know how the work was progressing.

Since I was both company secretary and project officer for this organisation and John McCarthy, the superintendent, was the chair of the board, there was a major church presence in the company. People at the meeting were enthusiastic about the aims of Chrysalis, but rather frightened of the huge costs being spoken off. Since they understood Chrysalis to be a church undertaking there was concern expressed by some as to how they could be expected to raise so much money. There was relief when it was explained that, although this was still a church-sponsored venture, the local church was not being asked to find more than they had always provided in finance.

Although there was a general acceptance that this should be a part of the deacon's work, several people raised concerns about the amount of time this would involve me in and how that would affect the pastoral oversight of the congregations.

Exhibitions

Homestart

Homestart lent me a ready-made exhibition on six panels. It came complete with a holder for leaflets and one for volunteer forms. This exhibition was put up in the entrance hall leading to the church halls and the back entrance to the church. It was in place for a full week and was seen by everyone who used the church during that period. At first we had intended to put up the exhibitions at the same time as we had the speakers, but later decided to keep the exhibition separate from the talks, and thus to extend the period of interest. Each exhibition was used at a time when I was delivering one of the sermons on the subject of diaconal ministry.

AIM, and the Drugs Work

The three display-panels that I was able to assemble about the work of the drugs related work consisted of leaflets and posters which, of themselves, did not make for an exciting display. However it was of sufficient interest to those using the church, both the congregation and other users, to cause them to read the information and to comment on it. Drugs related problems have a high profile on the Airedale estates and many of the older members were pleased to hear that there were people working with this problem. The use of the church premises for these associated activities met with general approval and I was able to offer help to both the Girls' Brigade and the Boys' Brigade with drugs education.

The Chrysalis Youth Project

The Chrysalis Youth Project had designed a presentation for use at a number of venues where they had been able to publicize what they were doing. This was readily offered for use in the church and, like the others, was in place for a week at Airedale. The display was of six panels consisting of photographs, an artist's impressions of the completed project and architects' drawings of the building. One of the young men from the project had made a large model of the site with buildings in place and the construction work complete. All of this attracted a great deal of attention and comment. Both the members of the fellowship group and the wider congregation were interested to know more about the Chrysalis Project and how it would operate. Almost everyone seemed to be supportive of its aims and anxious to know when building would start.

Venues

Each of these displays was also shown at Townville for a week. Unfortunately, because of its smaller size, Townville church does not lend itself to exhibitions in the way Airedale does. At Townville the exhibitions were in the worship area and were seen by both morning and evening congregations and, in each case, they were displayed at a time when I was delivering one of the related sermons. They were an effective aid in connecting the practical *diakonia,* in which the church was engaged, to the theological perspective presented in the sermons.

Two of the exhibitions were used at the largest churches in the other two sections of the circuit[33]. The Homestart exhibition went with me to Trinity Church in Castleford on the Sunday on which I used that sermon and stimulated a great deal of comment. Similarly I took the Chrysalis exhibition to Kippax. On this occasion I was to give a talk to the Kippax fellowship on an evening during the week. I chose to bring the exhibition with me and talk about my work, leaving the exhibition till the Sunday, so that it was on display when I delivered the sermon 'What is a Deacon for'.

Each of these away days was valuable in itself and raised the profile of the deacon's work in the circuit as a whole. As will be seen later this was fortunate and more valuable than we had originally realized.

In retrospect it is clear that the project worked in two parallel and complementary ways. My research gave a historical and theological perspective to the team's consideration of the deacon's role in *their* circuit. The discussion around the immediate role and the circuit's expectations provided a framework for my study of the deacon's ministry as a theological concept. My conclusions try to take account of both perspectives.

Part Two

Towards a Theological Perspective: The Research Project

Preface

Before we could answer the questions 'What should the deacon do?' and 'What is the difference between a deacon and a presbyteral minister?' we had to find out what a deacon is. There was only a limited and confused understanding of the deacon's ministry within the Methodist Church as a whole and practically none in the congregations of Airedale and Townville.

The theological basis for the project was informed by my programme of research. The discussions described in Chapter Four were based on some of the theological questions raised by this research. The team was initially given a brief outline of the historical development and theology of the diaconate but the conversations were centred on some of the ideas that I had gathered. This interaction provided a multidimensional viewpoint that I could not have achieved alone.

When I came to start the project I was aware that other denominations had a variety of understandings of the ministry of the deacon. It was also clear that those called to a permanent diaconate in other denominations were encountering similar difficulties.

The project needed to have a wider perspective than I could initially offer. If the team and the congregations were to do more than look at the situation from an insular or parochial viewpoint we needed to find out more about the ministry of the deacon as it was practised elsewhere and the traditions which lay behind it.

The three chapters that make up this part of the book outline the findings of this research. As was shown in Chapter Four the team and I started our discussions with a consideration of what the gospels tell us about *diakonia*. We then went on to look at the traditions and the different denominational developments. Chapter Five is a consideration of the biblical sources of the term deacon and the gospel uses of the related terms. This chapter firstly looks at the context in which the terms were used by the gospel writers and then the development of the use of the word deacon/diakonos to refer to someone who might have held a church office. Chapter Six describes the development and decline of the ordained diaconate in the early church and looks at the diaconate as re-instituted by the Reformers. Chapter Seven (the last of the research chapters) relates the upsurge of diaconal ministry amongst the Reformed churches in the early nineteenth-century and its expansion into Methodism by the later part of that century. The chapter also looks at the way the deacon's ministry has developed in a number of denominations throughout the twentieth century

This work offered me a wealth of new insights which have been helpful in understanding my call to the Methodist Diaconal Order. For the team there was an opportunity to step outside their immediate situation and think about why they had a deacon.

Chapter Five

Biblical Sources for Diaconal Ministry

Introduction

Despite being rooted in the earliest traditions of the church, diaconal ministry is not a clearly understood concept. There are almost as many definitions of this term as there are denominations. This is not simply a modern phenomenon, but would seem to have been true throughout most of the history of the Christian church. Within the biblical sources there are obvious variations in usage and understanding of the term and, as the church spread, these increased. There has probably been no time in history when the concept was generally agreed and understood.

Calvin's definition is one of the few that has a real claim to be theology. He characterized presbyteral ministry as being the fulfilment of the commandment of Jesus in Mark 12:30 which he sees as relating to worship[1], with diaconal ministry as the fulfilment of the second commandment, Mark 12.31 an expression of love or charity. It forms a neat, if debatable, line between presbyteral and diaconal ministry.

Biblical Sources and Church Traditions

Service and the servant in the gospels

The word *diakonia* (for ease of use I will use the transliterated Greek throughout) only appears once in the gospels and *diakonos* only eight times and not at all in Luke. It is the verb *diakoneo* which has the most frequent usage (appearing twenty-two times in all in eighteen verses) and in all four gospels.[2]

A clue to the way the word *diakonos* was understood by the writers of the gospels lies in Mark 9:35: 'If anyone wants to be first, he must be the very last, and the servant (*diakonos*) of all.' This story is told in all three of the synoptic gospels, but only Mark uses the servant term. Matthew speaks of being humble like a child, and Luke uses the phrase 'least among you'. But the illustration that Jesus is using of a child does not fit with the sense of 'table waiter' or 'least important'. As an illustration of Jesus's meaning it more clearly implies powerlessness, or someone who is under authority. His would seem to be the sense given to *diakonos* when it is used elsewhere in the gospels such as in Matt 22:13, where it is used of a king's attendants.

The other word in the servant group is *diakoneo* which is used widely throughout the gospels. Much of the difficulty we encounter in our interpretation of this word comes from our modern usage and the socio/political overtones we read into the word 'service'. *Diakoneo* is used in a number of situations, some of which can have the implication of menial work. If it were translated as 'cared for' it would convey its original meaning more clearly to the modern ear. An example of how translation into English can create quite different understandings of what is going on, is the story of the temptation of Jesus as told in Mark 1.13 and Matt 4.11. The NIV translated *diakoneo* as 'attended' in each case and the NRSV as 'waited on'. To the modern ear both of those terms come from the world of catering and only a few decades ago they would have suggested the servant's hall. In contrast the AV translates the word as 'ministered to'. Even today this terminology implies 'caring for' rather than menial labour. When the gospel stories are read with this latter meaning they make much more sense as a description of diaconal ministry.[3]

Service and the Concept of Deacon in other New Testament writings

Within the other New Testament writings these servant/service words have a more specific meaning than that used by the gospel writers. It is also within the translations of the New Testament epistolary writings that interpretation comes into play most vigorously as the translators attempt to fit the use of these terms to their understanding of 'minister'.

There are three Greek words that are important to the context of a study of the understanding of the deacon's ministry. The first of these is *diakonia* which is usually translated 'service', with the understanding that the original had overtones of table service. *Diakonia* appears in thirty-one verses in ten New Testament writings outside the gospels and is used thirteen times in the Epistles to the Corinthians alone.[4]

Next in frequency of use is *diakonos*, which appears in twenty verses but is never used in Acts. It is the word that we translate as 'deacon' when we refer to an office or title. It continues to be used this way in later church writings. The literal translation would seem to be servant, or waiter. John Collins[5] prefers the translation 'go-between' as giving more of the sense of how it was used by the society of the time. Along with this particular usage comes the idea of acting on behalf of, or performing a service at another's behest. This was one of the models that the team considered in Chapter Four.

The Greek word most widely used, even if only appearing fourteen times within this section of the New Testament, is *diakoneo*, 'to perform a service', 'to act as a servant', or 'to minister to', for which many translators offer the meaning 'to wait on someone at table'[6]. *Diakoneo* has been given a wide range of meanings by translators and, perhaps, has had most violence done to the sense of its original meaning in the attempt to make good English.

In the Book of Acts there is no use of *diakonos*. No one is given that title by the writer in any part of this work and most modern scholars are of the opinion that the origin of deacons is not to be found in Acts 6. Nor is there anything within Acts which is equivalent to the later understanding of deacon except, that is, the differentiation made between the two roles which is suggested in the text, the ministry of the word and the ministry of caring for the needy[7]. Although there has been discussion about the story of Acts 6 indicating a conflict between the Hellenists and the Hebrews this problem did not seem to have any involvement in the early attribution of diaconal precedents.[8]

From a very early stage in the life of the church, Irenaeus (c. 165) claimed Stephen as the first deacon and in the Canons of Neocaesarea[9] (c. 314 to 325) the seven in Acts are pointed to as the prototype for deacons. Whatever actually happened in Acts 6, it is important to ascertain the role that the first deacons were asked to fulfil.

In Acts 6.1 *diakonia* is generally understood as 'the daily distribution of food'. There is nothing in the text to make it clear that this is the precise 'service' that is being spoken of. This has to be inferred from the meaning of *diakonos*. This meaning includes the sense of waiting on tables which is the usual translation of *diakoneo* in verse 2, linked with *trapeza* meaning not only a table, but also a counting house. T. F. Torrance would suggest that the seven were in fact proto-presbyters, but nonetheless he says of deacons:

'So far as deacons are concerned, there was never any suggestion in the New Testament or in the early church that their office was restricted to the ministry of alms and care.[10]'

This would fit well with the understanding of the Church Fathers:

> 'The ministry of the deacon is not that of merely food and drink, but is the service of the Church of God.[11]'

That the 'service' inherent in the Acts 6:1 is about food and drink alone is not clear. That it was the service of the church is assured and that it was a work of charity would fit the context but that is as much as we can say with any certainty.

Collins suggests[12] that *diakonia* is equivalent to preaching (the ministry of the word) and he refers to Acts 20.24, 'However, I consider my life worth nothing to me, if only I may finish the race and complete the task the Lord Jesus has given me - the task of testifying to the gospel of God's grace.' and Acts 21.19, 'Paul greeted them and reported in detail what God had done among the Gentiles through his ministry' as evidence. The first text clearly speaks of a service of witnessing to the gospel and the second text refers to the results of Paul's *diakonia* amongst the Gentiles. Yet only a little earlier, in Acts 11.29, 'The disciples, each according to his ability, decided to provide *help* for the brothers living in Judea,' the text speaks of deciding to provide *diakonia* for the brothers living in Judea. In this context *diakonia* was not the ministry of the word. This variation of the meaning as used by one writer suggests that the context is crucial in our understanding of the meaning of this word and means that it would be unwise to be dogmatic in our interpretation of the term *diakonia*.

In Paul's letter to the Romans, both *diakonia*[13] and *diakoneo*[14] are used in the sense of a ministry of service. The context in Romans 12.7, 'If it is serving, let him serve; if it is teaching, let him teach;' makes this particularly clear. Here teaching and prophecy express the ministry of the Word in contrast to the ministry of service.

It is in Romans that we first encounter Paul's use of *diakonos*. It is only used three times, but these are important passages for our understanding. First, in Romans 13:4 we read 'For he is God's servant to do you good. But if you do wrong, be afraid, for he does not bear the sword for nothing. He is God's servant, an agent of wrath to bring punishment on the wrongdoer.' *Diakonos* is used here twice to mean 'someone who acts on behalf of God', and is reinforced, in the NIV translation, by adding the word 'agent'. As used in this passage *diakonos* has nothing to do with table service and does not refer to the ministry of the word, but is clearly seen to have an 'ambassadorial' connotation.[15]

Later in Romans 16:1, we read 'I commend to you our sister Phoebe, a servant of the church in Cenchrea.' There has always been dispute about the word *diakonos* here. Feminist scholars are sure it should read 'deacon' but those scholars opposed to the idea of Paul referring to a woman in ministry in the church, insist that Phoebe was a benefactress, not an official[16]. Paul's usage of *diakonos* in Chapter 13, above, might lead us to assume that Phoebe was at least an agent of the church, someone who was acting on its behalf. Of course, when put in its context, the passage follows the sending of Timothy into Thessalonia as Paul's *diakonos*[17] and it is in Timothy's churches that deacon is first seen used as a title.[18]

The use of the three diaconal words in the Corinthian epistles is so varied that it reinforces the contention that it is inappropriate to take one simple view on the use of the words, as though they were being used uniformly. It is obviously a more complex matter than that.

Paul uses *diakonos* six times in the Corinthian Epistles[19]. In all but one case it is clear from the context that he is talking about an agent, a servant who acts on behalf of someone, or something, else. The New Jerome Biblical Commentary[20] speaks of 'instrumental ministry' (1 Cor. 3.5), Paul 'mandated by God' (2 Cor. 3.6), servants of righteousness who 'do the work of

Satan' (2 Cor. 11.15) and of representing Christ (2 Cor 11.23. He uses *diakonia* thirteen times[21]. In almost all of these usages it is quite clear that he is speaking of a ministry of service:

> This service that you perform is not only supplying the needs of God's people but is also overflowing in many expressions of thanks to God. (2 Cor. 9.12)
>
> You know that the household of Stephanas were the first converts in Achaia, and they have devoted themselves to the service of the saints. (1 Cor. 16.15)

The New Jerome Biblical Commentary says of 1 Cor. 16.15 'Seeing a need, they met it. The basis of Christian authority is effective service to the community'.[22]

In Gal. 2.17 we read 'If, while we seek to be justified in Christ, it becomes evident that we ourselves are sinners, does that mean that Christ promotes sin? Absolutely not!' The NIV translates *diakonos* as 'promotes' whereas the NRSV as 'servant' while the RSV uses the translation 'agent' keeping the context of 'acting on behalf of' which is inherent in the other translations, if not as clearly stated. Clearly 'agent' is one of the principal meanings for *diakonia* in Paul's understanding.

The use of *diakonia* in Ephesians 4.12 refers to works of service to build up the church and it is set in the context of gifts of ministry, not of charity. It seems clear that Paul did not see those who carried out *diakonia* as mere waiters at table which a literal translation would suggest. As one works through the New Testament material, Collins' interpretation of the term *diakonia* as 'go-between' has much merit, and he goes on to provide a more complete understanding of the term as 'agent'.

It is in the First Epistle to Timothy that we first come upon the clear use of *diakonos* as a title.[24] *Diakonos* is used alongside the word for bishop, so it is clear that the author refers to two separate and different offices. Twice it appears this way[25] and then, in chapter 4.6, it is translated as minister.

The use of deacon as a title appears in one other place. That is in Paul's introduction to the Epistle to the Philippians (Phil 1.1). Some authorities see it as a reference to a function rather than a direct reference to an office, and the NRSV translates the terms for bishop and deacon as overseer and helper. *Diakonos* was the term Paul used when describing those he sent to work on his behalf. When he sent Timothy to Thessalonika he describes him, according to some of the early texts[26], as God's deacon. An interesting development is seen when Paul writes to Philippi on behalf of Timothy and himself: he refers to them both as servants, but uses the word *doulos* which means slave. On other occasions he would have used *diakonos* in this context. If the church at Philippi already had bishops and deacons as offices then *diakonos* would no longer fit his needs in that context.

The Judeo/Christian churches of Antioch and the Syrian area seemed to favour the term elder (*presbuteros*) as being more in the tradition to which they were accustomed. Paul and Barnabas appointed elders in all the churches they founded on that first missionary journey.[27] These elders seem to have been closely related to the courts of elders of the Jewish synagogues, and would thus fit comfortably into those churches from a Jewish background.[28] *Diakoneo* is the most widely used of this group of related words. It occurs in thirty-two verses within the New Testament, appearing in all the gospels and fourteen times in the epistles. Its context always implies serving others. How that 'service' is interpreted depends very much on the situation in which it is used. C. E. B. Cranfield[29] tells us that in Plato *diakoneo* is only considered as honourable when rendered to the state but its use in the New Testament seems to imply an honourable service rather than a servile one. In some ways I feel that the use of this word has an important bearing on the way we should understand its two sisters.

The most problematic usage of *diakoneo* is in Acts 6.2 where the NIV translates it as 'to wait on tables'. This could be a literal translation of the Greek phrase. This translation offers a clear understanding of bringing food and drink to others sat at the table but the rest of the story in which it is set does not seem to fit this concept. These 'waiters' are 'set aside' by the laying on of hands and prayer. The virtues required are spiritual and some go on to evangelize.[30] There is no clear answer to the difficulty this passage presents. This 'service of others' is contrasted with the service of the Word of God and this would seem to be the only time when serving God is not linked with serving others.

Linking an honourable serving of others with the service of God[31] makes a consistent sense of the usage throughout the New Testament. Despite its use in a variety of situations, understanding it in this way makes for a clear train of related ideas.

If *diakoneo* is understood as the service of others within a context of serving God, that understanding clarifies what we mean today in our use of *diakonia* as the service we offer within or on behalf of the church. In the same way we have a starting point for an understanding of *diakonos*/deacon as someone who serves God through the service of others. While this is still a much wider definition than a specific church office it offers a point of reference for our further consideration.

Chapter Six

From the Early Church to the Reformation

The Golden Age

The period from Ignatius of Antioch to the Council of Nicaea, the five centuries from 100 until 600 AD, has been referred to as 'the Golden Age of the diaconate'[1]. Despite the fact that the beginnings of the decline can be discerned as early as the fourth century, this is a time of growth and development of the diaconal ministry. It was the deacons' relationship to the bishops that brought about this decline in their fortunes. By the fourth century the rise in numbers, and the changing role of presbyters, created tensions that can be seen in the statements of some of the Councils[2] and the response of some presbyters to their situation.[3] It is almost certain that the changes that were taking place were regional at first, as would have been true of many of the changes happening to the church during this period[4]. It could be argued that the centralisation of power in Rome and the drive for unity of expression radically changed the growth pattern of the church.

At the very beginning of this time, c96 AD, Clement, the third Bishop of Rome, could write in his First Epistle to the Corinthians XLII.I.5[5]:

'So preaching in the country and city, they appointed their firstfruits, having tested them by the Spirit, to be bishops and deacons of those who should believe.'

At very much the same period of history, a mere ten years later perhaps, Ignatius writes from what is obviously a different tradition and a different place:

'Since therefore, I have been deemed worthy to behold you through Damas, your bishop, who is worthy of God, and your worthy presbyters Bassus and Apollonius and my fellow-servant the Deacon Sotion, of whom I have joy, because he is subject to the bishop as to the grace of God, and to the presbytery as to the law of Jesus Christ.[6]'

It would seem clear from these two examples that the church at Corinth was accustomed to bishops and deacons alone, while at Antioch and Magnesia they had bishops, presbyters and deacons. There has been much discussion as to the role of these Ignatian bishops, whether they were monarchical (autocratic) or monoepiscopal (presidential) with most authorities favouring the latter.[7] So the bishop was seen as a president of a council of elders/presbyters. Within this model the presbyter was a council member, a person of authority, but not at this time a holder of a liturgical function himself. The liturgical functions were vested in the bishop, elected to carry these out.

Separate from this group, were the deacons. Although it has been suggested that the council of elders could have included some deacons, there seem to be no references that actually point to a deacon acting as an elder. Some feel that it was at this time the beginning of the second century, when the Jewish Church and the Pauline churches came together to form a single body, into which both forms of ministry were grafted, with the council of elders having the ruling role but oversight being offered by a bishop who may have been first among equals at that time.[8] This union would not obviously alter the deacon's role in any significant way. Some commentators say that the deacon's role was one without any particular antecedents in either Judaism or elsewhere but grew out of the Christian experience.[9]

Whether there was any liturgical function invested in the deacon at this time is not always clear. It is likely that it was normal for there to be some, since Tertullian includes deacons with presbyters amongst those on whom the bishop might confer the power to baptize.[10] What is clear from a reading of the letters of Ignatius is that he himself held the deacon in high regard, speaking of deacons as his fellow servants, or 'those most dear to me'. While Ignatius is considered the father of the threefold order of ministry, he could not be said to be the father of the downgrading of the deacon to a lesser third order. Ignatius likens the deacon to Jesus Christ, the Bishop to God and the presbyters to the Apostles[11]. In a ranking such as that there is no obvious reason to assume a tiered hierarchy, rather a representative ordering with each ministry having its own value and all being subject to the community through the process of election and selection.

Another description of the early church by Justin Martyr offers a further insight into the deacon's position within that church:

'There is then brought to the president of the brethren bread and a cup of wine mixed with water; . . . those who are called by us deacons give to each of those present to partake of the bread and wine mixed with water over which the thanksgiving was pronounced, and to those who are absent they carry away a portion.[12]'

Once again there is reason to understand that the deacon had a set function and role within the liturgy. Justin does not mention bishop or presbyter, but the use of the term 'president of the brethren' suggests that we are encountering another term for bishop and elders.

It can be seen that the early church provides us with a variety of accounts of the deacon's role, and that during the second and third centuries deacons were respected ministers of the church with a definite liturgical role alongside the bishop. Deacons were considered to be successors to the seven in some way, if only in that they included in their role the oversight of alms, which had been understood to be the service of the seven in Acts 6.

By the fourth century we find a change in the way deacons are perceived by some presbyters. Jerome delivered a famous polemic against 'a mere server of tables', and Ambrosiaster writes of the inferiority of deacons in the following passage:

> 'The Apostle Paul proves that a presbyter is a bishop when he instructs Timothy, whom he had ordained as a presbyter, what sort of person he is to create a bishop. For what is a bishop but the first presbyter, that is, the highest priest? Finally, he calls these men none other than fellow presbyters and fellow priests. Does a bishop call his ministers fellow deacons? No, for they are much inferior, and it is a disgrace to mix them up with a judge (?). For in Alexandria and throughout Egypt, if a bishop is lacking a presbyter confirms (ordains?-*consignat*).[13]'

This period of conflict over the nature of the diaconate was to run over nearly 200 years as changes gradually took place in the Church. The various references to deacons in the Canons of the Councils at Arles and Nicaea indicate a pattern of withdrawal of rights and privileges from deacons. Wherever deacons were seen to be involved in what had come to be regarded as the role of the presbyter, this was to be forbidden:

> 'It has come to the knowledge of the holy and great Synod that, in some districts and cities, the deacons administer the Eucharist to the presbyters, whereas neither canon nor custom permits that they who have no right to offer should give the Body of Christ to them that do offer . . . let all such practices be done away.[14]'

Even as late as AD 625 the Quinsext Council complains of deacons with ecclesiastical office sitting above the presbyters at table.

It is important that we do not lose sight of the work of deaconesses in the early church. Apart from their role at baptism in supporting the female candidates, and assisting in the baptism proper, they performed much needed *charitable*[15] works of care. The move towards a hierarchical structure produced an unfortunate corollary, in that within the structures as within society at that time, women were not acceptable authority figures. This led, quite rapidly, to the disappearance of these roles for women in the western church.

The work of care which women deacons had been able to offer was fulfilled by the religious orders. For women there was soon no other way to offer service in the church than through entering a religious order. In the eastern churches, deaconesses continued to be a recognized ministry for some centuries after it was discontinued in the west. It was not until the eighth century that it slid into disuse, though the rite of ordination of deaconesses continued to appear in the Byzantine service books until the twelfth century[16].

A Vanishing Office

'Up to the fifth century the Diaconate flourished in the western Church, but after this period, it experienced, for various reasons, a slow decline which ended in its survival only as an intermediate stage for candidates preparing for priestly ordination.'[17] Other writers[18] on the subject would place the decline of the diaconate as a separate order from somewhere in the fourth century. Certainly, by the latter part of the fourth century, the idea of *cursus honorum*[19] had come into being and a clear hierarchical structure of church orders was in formation. There are records of hierarchical ordination and patterns of office in several parts of the church at about this time[20]. Equally clearly it was not a change that happened in all places at one time and we need to recognize that the church at this time came from different traditions and different cultures.

Despite acknowledging the evidence for a pluralistic church, many writers have worked from the premise that the church grew as a single organism, branching out as it developed and spread over an ever-greater area. A more helpful model is to understand the church as a group of families growing from a common ancestor, but separated by time and space. As the family grows it meets other families and together they tend to consolidate into a clan structure. Eventually several clans combine into one greater tribe and a new central set of rules predominate. A précis of this pattern of development is given in *The New Jerome Bible Commentary* and suggests that there was a universal pattern by the second century. However the quotation from the Canons of the Council of Nicaea, on p 113 above, would indicate that there were different patterns still in place at this time. The varying strands can be seen in the writings of several of the church fathers.[21]

As the Church in a given place developed the liturgical role of the presbyterate, and presbyters were changed from being councils of elders to undertaking some of the liturgical functions of the bishop, so the role of the deacon also changed. These changes may indicate an internal power struggle in the life of the church. The change of attitude towards deacons is perhaps best illustrated by two quotations.

'The deacons who are most dear to me, have been entrusted with the ministry of Jesus Christ who was with the Father before the world began.[22]'

These are the positive words of Ignatius of Antioch, but some 230 years later Jerome was able to say:

'I am told that someone has been mad enough to put deacons before presbyters, that is, before bishops. For when the apostle clearly teaches that presbyters are the same as bishops, must not a mere server of tables and widows be insane to set himself up arrogantly over men through whose prayers the body and blood of Christ are produced?[23]'

This power struggle ran over several centuries of change and can be seen in many aspects of the life of the Church. Before things began to change the deacon was an honoured assistant to the bishop, often acting for him, even in Councils. Eusebius, a deacon, represented Dionysius, bishop of Alexandria, at the Council of Antioch in 264. Athanasius played a leading part in the Council of Nicaea in 325 while still a deacon, before succeeding Alexander as bishop[24]. Through the third and fourth centuries there were still important roles for deacons to play, although the comments of Jerome, written circa AD340, indicate this was not a universal situation.

The Transitional Deacon

By the end of the fifth century the hierarchical system had become so clearly codified that there can be little doubt that deacons had ceased to have a separate identity in most parts of the church. In the western church in particular the position and role of the deacon changed and was gradually subsumed into that of the presbyter.[25] By the tenth century the diaconate was almost solely a probationary step for those intending for the priesthood. This had real consequences for the deacon's role and had, in practice, removed the third order from the ministry. If all those who were ordained deacon had no intention of serving as deacon, had no call to this particular ministry, but were intended for the priesthood, then 'the sacrament exists only as a sham'[26]. John StH. Gibaut continues

'What does the transitional diaconate mean? At best it is a polite fiction, at worst pious fraud. In almost every ordination of a person in transit, there exists a defect of intention. Transitional deacons don't intend to be deacons. They intend to be priests. Nor does the church intend them to be deacons . . . one must intend the order, and the church must intend it. Not for convenience. Not as a rite of passage into a new status in the church. But as a lifelong commitment to an order which finds it's meaning in the imaging of service, the diaconate of Christ.[27]'

The consequence for the church was the loss of the symbol and the representation that the deacon had provided. The gradual assumption by the presbyters of some of the traditional functions of the deacon and the assumption by the presbyterate of the title 'Archdeacon' demonstrate the absorption of this once distinctive ministry. Kevin Flynn describes how the symbolic role of the deacon in the liturgy has been lost and its effect on the representative *diakonia.*[28]

This claim to hold all the offices and ministry of the church within one person seems to offend against the Pauline view of the Church as the body of Christ. The idea that all the charisms were to be valued and that each in his/her place made up the whole body had been replaced by a view in which all ministry was contained in one person.

Function and Role in the Early Middle Ages

We now consider the functions of the deacon as they have developed in the wider ministry of the church.

The administrative and charitable functions of the diaconate had included acting as the bishop's go-between, or ambassador, administering the charity of the church. Jill Pinnock lists the following liturgical functions for the deacon, i.e. to lead prayers at the Eucharist, to convey the people's offerings to the priest, to distribute Communion to the people, to read the gospel, and occasionally to preach.[29] The charitable functions remaining to the diaconate by the end of the fourth century were much reduced, but there were still deacons who administered church properties and some archdeacons (in deacon's orders) who acted as assistants to the bishop.

There were rare and exceptional deacons who kept to their vocation, for example Francis of Assisi in the thirteenth century, who remained a deacon throughout his life[30]. In the fifteenth century Cardinal Piccolomini administered the diocese of Siena as a deacon for forty years until his election to the papacy in 1503[31]. Some fifty years later Cardinal Reginald Pole, one of the three presidents of the Council of Trent, was still in deacon's orders at that time and remained so until being made bishop later[32].

These exceptions notwithstanding, the norm during this period was of a swift transitory period as deacon, usually twelve months, but occasionally less, and then ordination as a presbyter. These two ordinations were separated only by a short space of time.[33]

So what had happened to those functions which were still considered diaconal? In the absence of a deacon, and this was in most cases, all of the liturgical functions were carried out by a presbyter acting as deacon. The practical situation often was that, in a large church with a congregation to match, there would be several presbyters available, perhaps even a bishop also. They would divide the roles amongst themselves, some performing the roles of deacons and some of presbyters, while at Easter with large numbers to be confirmed it would not be unusual to find bishops fulfilling all three roles.[34]

The first function of the deacon lay in a concern with charitable works. However, it was not the deacon's responsibility to *do* the charitable work of the church, rather to act as a focus for the charitable work of the whole people of God. Within that function were many minor roles, such as the administration of charitable trusts, the care of church properties, and the distribution of alms. Central to the role was the function of 'being accessible'. Although most current research claims that the origins of the diaconate are not to be found in the text of Acts[35], the model presented by Luke is clearly part of the early church's understandings of the deacon's role:

'The deacons are to act as intermediaries for the bishop, and the people are to have very free access to the deacons, and let them not be troubling the head at all times.[36]'

The deacon had to be available to the congregation and to respond to needs through the agency of the congregation rather than through the bishop:

'They are to learn of the sick and 'bring them to the notice of the multitude,' not the bishop, so that the people of the Church may visit them and supply their needs as the bishop thinks necessary.[37]'

Their role was to receive appeals from the congregation on behalf of individuals and to enable the congregation to make their own response.

During the Middle Ages the office of deacon had become the third order in the threefold order of ministry and was seen as the stepping stone to the priesthood. By the twelfth century the diaconate had little to call its own and its charitable role had ceased to have significance as part of the office. This was largely due to a theological shift:

'Mediaeval theologians appraised the spiritual works of mercy higher than the corporeal, seeing that the spirit is more noble than the flesh[38]'

This view changed the focus of the church's charity that was seen in terms of absolution. Priests were attached to the hospitals and offered to hear confessions and give communion to those in need.

The Reformation

By the middle of the sixteenth century Calvin's diatribe against the deacons of his day was brought about by the fact that they had become purely minor functionaries at the liturgy.[39] But his criticism does suggest that there were some who remained in deacons' orders at this time.

Luther and some of his fellow Reformers recognized only one ministerial office, the ministry of the Word and Sacrament. For Luther in particular, there was no higher calling than that of preaching the Word. Bishops and presbyters were all representatives of one ministry with differing commissions. From this perspective pastoral work could be left to others such as the diaconate, who were a lower order of ministry not entrusted with preaching the Word.

Luther's difficulty with deacons stems from what they had become, not what he understood them to be. It was the liturgical role into which the deacon of his day had slipped that Luther despised[40]. He called those who carried it out a plague on the church,[41] and claimed that 'The diaconate . . . is a ministry for distributing the Church's bounty to the poor, in order that priests may be relieved of pastoral concerns'[42].

This was a time when the idea of poverty[43] as Christian perfection had become a powerful force, particularly within the church in Germany. It was this situation which caused Luther to advocate the establishment of the parish chest[44]. Luther was particularly incensed by the sight of a bishop sitting outside his palace begging and felt that the proliferation of mendicant friars and monks harmed the real poor.

Luther's deacons were lay people with an understanding of their role based on Acts 6, with the distribution of alms. Calvin, Bucer and most of the Reformers were very concerned with social works and the diaconal community which was for them the church,[45] but all were influenced by their need to give pre-eminence to the Word. This seemed to compel them to place diaconal ministry entirely in the realm of the laity. This system, and what they asked of it, was not a problem as long as they were able to operate effective systems of social care, but, when the economy of the area took a downturn, the systems failed to operate and there was no representative ministry to provide a focus which could respond to the changed circumstance. The deacon had become an administrator with no ministry role or vision.[46]

For Calvin there were four *orders* of ministry (pastor, teacher, elder and deacon) but only two *forms* of ministry, presbyteral and diaconal[47]. The first three of these were ordained presbyters carrying out different functions and the deacon was a lay minister. In general this division was upheld by all the Reformed churches. The hierarchical[48] concept of ministry with its threefold order is the only other model which has held any real sway in the church. This model has dominated the behaviour of the episcopal churches since the eighth century[49], although it first developed in the fourth century[50]. Calvin seems to have appointed his five Geneva deacons as administrators of the secular relief agencies already operating in the city with the intention of bringing these agencies under religious authority.[51]

From its foundation the Church has found it necessary to focus and refocus its ministerial response to the two great commandments, Mark 12:30-31, according to the circumstance in which it has found itself. The events of Acts 6 can be seen as one of the first such circumstance. Calvin places the beginning of the diaconate with this event[52] in which he sees the Apostles as struggling to respond to the Great Commission (Matt 28:11-20), in a situation where the Christian community is failing in its response to the second of Jesus's commandments (Mk 12:31).

For the next few centuries there would be little change in the place of deacons within the churches. In the Roman Catholic Church and the Church of England the office was used as the first step towards priestly status. In both churches, however, there were those who remained deacons even if their motives had little to do with valuing the office. Deacons were clergy who had no ecclesiastical responsibilities. It was an office used by university professors and church administrators who required a clerical status but did not want the responsibilities of priesthood.

Chapter Seven

Nineteenth-Century Experiments and the Contemporary Scene

The Nineteenth-Century Orders

During the nineteenth century 'Many Christians believed that they must take responsibility for social welfare in a Europe suffering from war and urbanisation'.[1] Throughout Europe there were a variety of responses to the problems which the French Revolution and the Napoleonic wars brought to the continent, and there was a great upsurge in the activity of the religious orders. The women's orders in particular made great changes, becoming less enclosed and entering the work of nursing and teaching with great enthusiasm.[2] The following are some of the exciting experiments in diaconal ministry during this time, even if diaconal terminology was not always used.

The Bruderhaus

In 1833 Johann Hinrich Wichern founded a home for vagrant boys in Hamburg. This was part of a Sunday School enterprise intended to educate and safeguard children. He gathered the children into groups of about a dozen under the care of a 'Bruder' and they received basic education and practical help, as well as training in simple trades, such as tailoring and shoemaking. By 1839 Wichern had founded a Bruderhaus[3] to educate and train the Brothers who would go out into the slums and jails. Wichern did not use the term deacon for these men, however, continuing with the term Brother.

The Lutheran Deaconesses at Kaiserwerth

An order of deaconesses was founded in 1836 at Kaiserwerth by Pastor Fliedner of the German Evangelical Church. It was initially comprised of single women, who were involved in nursing and pastoral work, and has been recognized 'as the most significant establishment of a trained and maintained diaconal order'.[4]

Fliedner had first become involved with social and charitable work as a young pastor. He began visiting prisons and, through his work, regular prison chaplaincy began in Germany. Fliedner moved on to the provision of a half-way house for released women prisoners, and an extension of the half-way house was the founding of a nursery school that eventually became a school for future teachers.

Shortly after starting this work he encountered deaconesses amongst the Moravians[5]. As he became more and more involved in this sort of work he came to feel that the order of deaconesses should be revived within the Lutheran Church and he opened a hospital and deaconess training centre[6]. By 1838 he was already able to send deaconesses to another hospital and the order flourished. Deacon houses were also established at this time, although they were often not as successful. Some of the deacons of the Fliedner orders were principally administrators, as society generally would not accept women in positions of authority and it was often necessary to appoint men as administrators for the houses and the hospitals.

In 1849 Dr William Passavant of the Lutheran Church in America met Fliedner and persuaded him to send four deaconesses to Pittsburgh to work in the Pittsburg Infirmary. A member of Passavant's congregation offered her services to the deaconesses and in 1850 Sister Louisa Martens was consecrated as the first American deaconess. Sister Louisa worked as a deaconess for 50 years and established hospitals and homes for orphans from Philadelphia in the east to Chicago in the west. She also founded the Silver-Springs-Martin Luther School in Pennsylvania that is still working today.

Fliedner was busy opening deaconess houses in many other centres such as Jerusalem in 1851 and Paris and Berlin shortly after. By the time of his death in 1864 there were thirty motherhouses[7] and 1,600 deaconesses world-wide.

From the beginning the Kaiserwerth deaconesses were not a church-based order, and, initially, the institutional church took no part in their work. There is a sense in which it could be said that all of this work took place despite the churches with which it was associated. The deaconesses were not considered able to administer their own affairs and so they had male administrators to control the houses. Even though the houses had a Sister Superior and the Sisters undertook all training, there was a perceived need for a male hand controlling the finances and the links with the churches themselves. After a few years the Evangelical (Lutheran) Church in Germany consecrated the deaconesses and owned them in an institutional manner but did not take administrative ownership. The deaconess houses were always separate from the churches and did not have any real connection with the church as an organisation. Support from the church was most often from individual church persons, rather than from the congregations as a whole.

There was never any attempt to provide a liturgical role for the deaconesses of the Lutheran Church in Germany or in America, nor would Fliedner or Passavant have considered this as a necessary or desirable part of the role of the deaconess. The work was always of a charitable and social nature. While the work with prisoners and the nursery schools continued, leading to the training of chaplains and nursery school teachers, Kaiserwerth quickly became a training school for nurses. It would seem that this was the first organized training scheme for nurses and became the pattern for Lutheran deaconess work throughout the world.

The Lutheran Church in Sweden

The first deaconess house in Sweden was founded at Ersta in 1851 under the influence of the German Lutheran Church.[8] Such diaconal institutions were founded by individual, parish based societies and were seen principally as part of the charitable work of the church. At this time the diaconal role was considered to be part of the responsibility of the priest and 'one of the vows for the ordination of priests had a clear charitative (sic) character until 1987'[9].

Uniquely within the Lutheran tradition, the churches in Sweden and Denmark continued with a hierarchical mode of ministry with Bishops and Priests, and the Swedish Church maintained a liturgical function for the deacon into the seventeenth century. Although the diaconal order disappeared at this time, it was the terms 'deaconess' and 'deacon' which were used two hundred years later for the new orders, which set up first at Ersta and then later in other Houses throughout the country. These deacons and deaconesses acted as the local churches' arm for social work at a time when the administrative format for the country was the parish, and the social and charity work was left to the local church authorities. In Sweden the Deaconess houses became the responsibility of the local church from the beginning and this has remained a feature of the Scandinavian style since.

The Lutheran Church in Norway

The first deaconesses came to Norway in 1868 with the foundation of the House of Deaconesses. This deaconess's house was joined shortly after by *Diakonhjemmet,* The Deacons' Home, which was founded to train men for works of love and charity in areas where women were not deemed able to participate: e.g. the care of alcoholics, prisoners and the mentally ill. The *Diakonjhemmet* College was founded in 1890 and the hospital was opened in 1893.

The United Methodist Church

The Methodist Episcopal Church in America had established itself in Germany in the 1850s, and in 1874 founded a deaconess order after the Kaiserwerth pattern. This example was quickly exported back to North America where, under the influence of Lucy Rider Meyer, it began to spread rapidly. One change that took place in America was that the deaconesses were less confined to the institutions. Although there were deaconess houses and centres, the individual deaconesses went out into the communities and developed their work in the community.

While the Lutheran church had the high cost of establishing hospitals and schools to consider, if its impact was to be significant, the American Methodist model meant that many of the deaconesses worked and lived in the community which they sought to serve.

The British Methodist Church

The advent of deaconess work within the British Methodist Church was gradual and not the idea, or plan, of one person, though Thomas Bowman Stephenson is credited with the introduction of deaconess work into the Methodist Church in Great Britain. In 1867 Stephenson was serving at Bolton where he started work among children and women. He did this through employing a Mrs Entwhistle, whom he called deaconess. This was a completely personal arrangement and had no formal church recognition. In 1869 Stephenson was sent to Lambeth, London, where, with the aid of two generous supporters, Alfred Mager and Francis Horner, he set up a home for orphaned and homeless children. In 1873 Stephenson was appointed Principal of the Children's Home, a post which he held for the next 27 years until a bout of ill health compelled him to give this work up for a spell.

Methodism was still a divided Church at this time and, in the United Methodist Free Church, the Rev. T. J. Cope opened a Training House for deaconesses called Bowron House in 1891. Deaconesses were trained for what was to be called the Deaconess Order. In the Primitive Methodist Church the Rev. T. J. Flanagan founded a sisterhood whose members were never called deaconesses, but were part of the Home Mission Department of the Church.

Quite early in the life of the Children's Home Stephenson encouraged the older girls to remain at the home and undertake training, These he called Sisters of the Children and they were the first of the National Children's Home Sisters[10]. Stephenson continued with work in the community through the employment of women in other ways, but the Children's Home occupied most of his spare energies for a few years.

In 1886 the Rev. Peter Thompson, the founder of the East London Mission, formed a sisterhood and in West London the Rev. Hugh Price Hughes did the same. Neither of these groups was called deaconess, although the term 'Sister' was used, not only by these two, but by others. The Revs George Clegg and S. F. Collier, and Miss Mary Champness all had groups of women called sisters working in a variety of social ministries within the church in their own areas. There was no co-ordinated effort to make any official organisation to cover all this work and this almost brought about a clash between two of the main proponents at the time:

> 'Through the columns of the 'Methodist Times', the Rev. Hugh Price Hughes indicated that he was thinking of starting a training project for his own Sisters of the Poor. This surprised Dr. Stephenson, because he knew that Mr. Hughes was aware that he had a similar project in mind for the whole Church. In the same year Dr. Stephenson wrote a little book, 'Concerning Sisterhoods.' In this work he laid down three principles: there must be vocation, but no vow; there must be discipline but no servility; there must be association, not excluding freedom.[11]'

Stephenson must have been a very persuasive man, for in that year he received a donation of £500 from a friend, William Mewburn, which he used to open the first training home. Mewburn House opened in 1890, and the first services for the 'setting aside' of the Sisters of the Children and the Sisters of the Poor, took place in 1891. At first the Wesleyan Methodist Church left the whole project in private hands while giving it support, and by 1894 there were 44 deaconesses in the circuits. Hugh Price Hughes' project is never heard of again and in 1895 the Conference of the Wesleyan Methodist Church gave recognition to what it now called the Wesley Deaconess Institute. In 1901 it became a department of the Church.

Stephenson's first intention seemed to be to use the deaconesses in the same way he had used his less formal women assistants. For this they received training in medical care and home economics. He had been impressed by the work of the Kaiserwerth deaconesses when he had gone to visit Fliedner. But he had also had some communication with the Methodist

Episcopal deaconesses in America and seems to have been influenced by their different approach. The training offered at Mewburn House included not only basic medical care and childcare, but theology and hermeneutics. The prospectus that Stephenson quotes in *Concerning Sisterhoods*, shows a very different focus[12]. The Wesley deaconesses were intended to be a mobile mission force who could be sent wherever they were needed. The young women who came to Mewburn were from good homes and had to bear part of the cost of the training themselves. They were thrown into the deep end from the beginning as they were expected to go out in pairs to work in the East End of London.

The first Wesley deaconess left the country for work abroad as early as 1894. Sister Evelyn Oates sailed out to Durban in March of that year, and worked there for a short spell before moving to Johannesburg where she replaced a South African deaconess who had worked there for eighteen months previously. That there was a deaconess in South Africa at all demonstrates how the idea had taken hold, and her story illustrates some of the diversity of the deaconess movement:

In 1890 the Rev. R. Fuller Applebe answered the Manse door to a caller with a remarkable story, she was a woman who had been brought up a Roman Catholic and until recently had worked for the church as a nurse. She had been through a period of doubt and prayer and fasting and had as a result of that been able to find a great release from sin, but also a new direction. She had just arrived in Johannesburg and wanted to work for the Protestant church. Applebe accepted her offer and, apparently on his own authority, ordained her as a Wesley Methodist Deaconess and set her to work in the gold fields. He built for her a tiny tin cottage where she worked for eighteen months until she suddenly died. Her headstone bears the inscription. 'Sister Theresa: Wesleyan Deaconess, a healer of the sick and a friend of the friendless: lover of little children.'[13]

At the same time there were calls for deaconesses from the Methodist Church and missionary societies in other parts of the world. New Zealand, Ceylon (Sri Lanka) and India were all asking for deaconesses urgently and by the beginning of the 1900s West Africa and China were also interested.

Sister Christian Hughes was sent to New Zealand and set up the first Deaconess House in Dunedin. Houses were opened in Wellington and Christchurch and deaconesses trained there. By 1908 there were Wesley deaconesses from both the British Order and from the New Zealand Church working in different centres in New Zealand. Much of the work undertaken by the deaconesses was amongst the poor working classes, and in combating the harmful effects of drunkenness amongst the white agricultural workers and the Maoris.

There were deaconesses working and training in Australia at this time. Some had been trained in Britain and some in the new houses set up Brisbane and Sydney. One deaconess, Sister Isabel Sinclair, had the task of going from township to township in the bush, collecting 'The Daily Bread Mission Boxes'. She preached and held services everywhere she went, and this at a time when women were not normally permitted to be local preachers in the Wesleyan Church.

With the advent of this mission work, the young women coming into training were being selected with great care. They were also being asked to be qualified in some specialist field before they were accepted for training. The deaconesses sent abroad had to have skills as nurses, teachers, or midwives, so that they would be of practical help. They were also trained to preach and teach the gospel. The methodology followed by the deaconesses was: first to present God's love and grace in a practical way, and then explain why they did such a thing, when they would offer an opportunity to learn about the gospel.

At the Wesley Deaconess convocation of 1896 Mrs Trimmer, the wife of a Wesleyan Missionary in Ceylon, made an appeal for deaconesses to be sent to Puttur, where she hoped that they might act as missionaries to the women of the area. Convocation took up the challenge and it was decided to send two deaconesses out to Ceylon. There was no funding for the stations and the only way that it was possible was if the deaconesses supported it themselves. This they pledged to do, and from 1897 to 1964 this is just what they did. The Ceylon mission was a Wesley Deaconess mission and at times there were six to eight deaconesses in Ceylon. They trained 'Biblewomen'[14] and then Singhalese and Tamil deaconesses. At this time the cost to a circuit of a deaconess, including accommodation, was £50 per year and it was out of this small income that the British deaconesses funded all this work. An example of their work is shown in this extract from a letter to the warden, the Rev. W. R. Maltby:

'One great feature of the year's work has been the admission of six candidates for training in Christian work to the Training House in Puttur, in response to an appeal issued by the Synod to the Churches of the District, early in the year. The curriculum includes Bible Study, Hygiene, Home Nursing, Domestic Science and Infant Maternal Welfare. The students have also trained in practical work, and during their first five months have visited 487 homes, taught 3,210 women and 5,130 children, and taken part in 106 organised meetings.[15]'

The style and range of work being undertaken by the Wesley Deaconess Order was obviously different from that of the Kaiserwerth deaconesses from whom the inspiration had sprung.

Patterns and Styles

While all the records indicate that Fliedner's movement had a huge influence in the growth of the deaconess orders, it was more inspirational than formative. Although the deaconesses of the United Methodist Church first appeared in Germany, neither they, nor the British deaconess orders, seem to have followed the style of the Lutheran deaconesses.

What seems to have happened during this revival of diaconal ministry is that two different church backgrounds, with two separate theologies and with differing roots, set out from a shared vision. In the Lutheran case the diaconal model was shaped by a tight theology of ministry and in the Methodist by a looser theology of ministry which allowed a freedom to do almost whatever they could imagine, as long as they could fund it.[16]

All this revived diaconal ministry may have had the same spiritual launching pad, but it developed in a variety of directions. The tightly restricted vision of the German Lutheran church moved out through the Scandinavian Lutheran churches, with a doctrine of ministry somewhere between the German churches (one ministry, several roles) and the Church of England's episcopal threefold ministry. The movement spread rapidly through the energy of the United Methodists in Germany and America and a wide variety of traditions were rediscovered, with perhaps the greatest freedom in the Methodist Church in Britain where experiment and initiative were allowed free rein. All of this has meant that the twentieth century developments have had a greatly varied set of parameters from which to choose when trying to establish, or re-establish, their diaconal personae.

If the seven individuals mentioned in Acts chapter 6 were deacons, then they were in the Fliedner model of charitable care. British Methodism had moved to Acts 8:12 which included the wider role of Philip, 'But when they believed Philip as he preached the good news of the kingdom of God and the name of Jesus Christ, they were baptized, both men and women.'[17]

Diakonia Today – a Vision and an Opportunity

Since the 1950s theologians from a range of traditions have spoken of diaconal ministry in terms of a hope for the future, and an opportunity for the church. Barnett makes an important point about looking back:

> 'The renewal of the diaconate envisioned here involves no less than its restoration as a full and equal order. This does not, of course, mean a reconstruction of the office as it was in the early Church but rather its renewal in the modern world to serve the Church in terms of our own day and our particular needs. The deacon will again be the symbol par excellence of the servant-Christ and the whole mission of service given by him to us his people. The office of the deacon will then again be the measure by which all ministry is taken, it being the representative form of the whole.[18]'

Barnett writes from the viewpoint of an Anglican and an American. He has caught a vision, one that he feels needs to be shared with the whole of his church. He has interpreted *diakonos* as minister, but in an entirely different sense from John Collins[19]. Barnett sees minister in the sense of the whole ministry of Christ, while Collins understands it as the particular ministry of the Word as represented by the presbyter[20]. In Barnett's terms there is an understanding of the deacon's ministry as representative, representing Christ to the church and the world in such a way that it focuses each Christian's own ministry.

His view is not universally held, but would seem to be increasingly representative of today's thinking. Different churches are making statements about diaconal ministry today which, although coming from different directions, are starting to point in one.[21] Diaconal ministry has come to the forefront of discussion in many of the churches in the world, and huge steps have taken place in the last few years. So much so that, writing in the original preface to Barnett's book in 1981, Reginald Fuller could say that the Roman Catholic Church still saw the diaconate as a stepping stone to the priesthood, but the 1996 statistics from the National Conference of Catholic Bishops in the United States lists 21,873 deacons in 123 countries world-wide, with 45 archdioceses in the United States having 7500 permanent deacons serving.[22]

The Catholic Church

There have been changes of style, of understanding, and of acceptance in most of the churches where the diaconate exists and major changes have come about in the last ten years or so. As already indicated, the Roman Catholic position has undergone some major changes in the last few years. There are permanent deacons working in parishes throughout the United Kingdom: the figures for January 1996 show 360, and this seems to be a growing vocation.

'Throughout history the service of deacons has taken on various forms so as to satisfy the diverse needs of the Christian community and to enable the community to exercise its mission of charity. It is for the bishops alone, since they rule and have charge of the particular Churches 'as Vicars and legates of Christ', to confer ecclesiastical office on each deacon according to the norm of law. In conferring such office, careful attention should be given to both the pastoral needs and the personal, family (in the case of married deacons), and professional situation of permanent deacons. In every case it is important, however, that deacons fully exercise their ministry, in preaching, in the liturgy and in charity to the extent that circumstances permit. They should not be relegated to marginal duties, be made merely to act as substitutes, nor discharge duties normally entrusted to non-ordained members of the faithful. Only in this way will the true identity of permanent deacons as ministers of Christ become apparent and the impression avoided that deacons are simply lay people particularly involved in the life of the Church.[23]'

In the United States it would be rare for a diocese not to have serving deacons. This trend is clearly seen throughout the world, if more emphatically so in the developed countries.

'The second Vatican Council prepared the Church for the restoration of the permanent diaconate. The deacon was once more to play an important part in the life of the Church, not just as a temporary ministry for candidates being ordained to the priesthood.[24]'

If the diaconate was to play an important part in the life of the church, what was that part to be and how was it to be understood? First, '(the deacon) is no longer a layman nor can he return to the lay state'.[25] He lives within the community, he is not separated out but is drawn from the community which he serves. The understanding of the Catholic Church about the permanent diaconate is laid down in the document *Sacrum Diaconatus Ordinum* (June 18, 1967). This is still in the process of being put into practice at the local level, but the document gave bishops the freedom to ordain permanent deacons while not obliging them to do so. This has meant that many bishops have chosen to opt out of the possibility of a permanent diaconate for most of that time, The growth over the intervening years has been patchy. In 1997 the diocese of Liverpool had eighty deacons but the diocese of Hallam (Sheffield) had none and there was only one permanent deacon in Ireland.

Wherever the diaconate is taken seriously, it brings surprises to the priests who become involved and offers new insights into the laity's attitudes. When the new Bishop of Hallam appointed the Rev. Brian Green to be the director of the permanent diaconate in 1997, Brian approached the matter with some misgivings. He worried about how the lay people would understand what was happening, and whether they would not simply see it as an extension of clericalism. Brian was surprised by the response when he got into discussion:

'This is really just where we are at,' one of them commented. 'We have developed a lot of ministries in the parishes - catechists, ministers of Reader and of the Eucharist, ministries of administration and care and so on. What we need now is some further possibility for people who are still in the world, married, able to support themselves, but are feeling called to an even deeper involvement in ministry. Deacons could be the next step in that development.'[26]

Owing to the varying pace of development of these ideas in parishes and dioceses it is often difficult to see what exactly is happening within the local Roman Catholic dioceses, but some are developing a wide-ranging lay involvement.

Recent writing on the ministry of the deacon in the Roman Catholic Church is varied, but there is a fairly common theme. A representative example from the Diocese of Lake Charles in the United States tells us:

'They preside at sacraments. They witness the sacrament of Matrimony. They perform the sacrament of Baptism. They preside at wake, funeral and committal services.

Their ministries are as varied as are their talents. Some are involved in pro-life ministry, some in serving the poor, minorities, incarcerated, and the nursing home or home bound. They teach, evangelize.[27,]

With the falling interest in the vocations to the religious life and even to the priesthood[28], it seems that the ministry of the deacon is coming back into its own. The role it fulfilled in the early church was so important a part of the church's task, that a multitude of different responses and vocations had to be set up, as the deacon's role became merely a temporary and titular part of the priest's omnivorous[29] role. Today, as the church struggles with dwindling vocations, both in the third and the first world, the deacon's role comes into focus again.

The Anglican Communion

For many years, particularly in the 1980s, the discussion about a permanent diaconate was confused by its connection with the question of the ordination of women. A great deal of the writings that poured forth from the Church of England dealt with the subject almost exclusively from the point of view of the appropriateness of women in the priesthood. Now that this has been dealt with it would seem that there should be room for a more open discussion of the subject, and for progress to be made in this matter. The starting points for the discussion are, however, rather shaky.

It has been said that the Church of England believes in a threefold ministry 'of Bishops, Priests and Readers'[30]. The report to the House of Bishops in 1988 shares some of this ambivalence to the diaconate:

'215 *Distinctive Deacons* are seen as having a very similar role to the professional Accredited Lay Worker but stand within the ordained ministry and have additional liturgical functions. It remains unclear how this order will develop, as many of the women who now make up the order see their vocation ultimately as to a priestly and not to a diaconal ministry.[31]'

This statement is placed in order of discussion, after the description of accredited lay workers and readers. It would certainly seem from this sort of statement that 'Distinctive Deacons' are not actually understood as the same thing as deacons in a threefold ministry. There are dioceses that have no permanent deacons and even some where the bishop would actively discourage a candidate from remaining in that order. The Rev Stanley Baxter, an Anglican priest (married to Elizabeth who was first a deaconess, then ordained deacon and finally ordained priest) suggested this was because they would have no position in which to place them. He suggested the diocese of Portsmouth, which has 30 permanent deacons and a vigorous formation of diaconate course, as an example of a more informed response in this respect.

The ecumenical dimension would seem to be having a direct influence on the progress of the thinking about the diaconate. Perhaps one of the most important outcomes is the discussion of the Anglican-Lutheran International Commission. The position of these two churches on the threefold ministry has long been a point of discussion between them. What is clear from the report is that the more polarized views, represented by the Church of England and the German Evangelical Church, were bridged to a great extent by the more flexible approaches of the overseas Anglican communions and the Nordic and American Lutheran churches. Only in this way could the following statement have been produced:

'66.   Thus, for instance, Lutheran churches without an ordained diaconate are challenged to consider whether such a diaconate as has been described above (including a liturgical grounding in the ministry of Word and sacrament) would be of value in their service of the gospel and, if so, whether a diaconal ministry more reflective of the practice of the wider church and Christian tradition could appear as a legitimate development for Lutherans.

67.   Anglican churches are challenged to restore to the diaconate (as defined above) its character as a lifelong and distinct form of ordained ministry, including with its liturgical function a pastoral focus on *caritas* and *justitia* in church and society. Such a restoration would imply both a reconsideration of the transitional diaconate and the possibility of direct ordination to the priesthood of persons discerned to have presbyteral vocations without their 'passing through' the diaconate. The possibility of such direct ordination is not excluded on historical or theological grounds.

68.   In both traditions, the presbyters may perceive a renewed diaconate as a threat to their own identity and role. This will be especially so where the presbyteral office is seen as the embodiment of all ordained ministry. If, however, presbyters can welcome deacons as partners-in-ministry, both liturgically and within the church□s mission, then they may themselves be freed to exercise a more focused ministry, bearing responsibility for the life of the community in Word and sacrament. In this way, too, the diaconate can stand as a witness against the perennial threat of clericalism, an ecclesiastical distortion rooted in exclusivist attitudes and practices. Deacons are called by the very nature of their order to stand as a witness to presbyters and bishops that the authority of all ordained ministry is for service alone.[32]'

Four major changes have occurred in the pattern of diaconal ministry in the Episcopal Churches of North America over the last 150 years. In the 1840s men, ordained as deacons, were sent to serve as missionaries to isolated communities and to the North American Indians. This work continued through into the 1930s. In 1885 the deaconess order was formed and they were set apart, by prayer and the laying on of hands by a bishop, to work with the sick, the poor and the needy. In 1952 the church took the bold step of ordaining men as perpetual deacons to serve within parishes as pastoral and sacramental assistants. These last were mainly older men.

In 1970 the deaconess orders stopped recruiting and the church, in 1971, ordained both men and women as deacons, with a liturgical base within the church and a social work base outside it. Some of these deacons serve the church in a full-time capacity such as archdeacon or educational specialist.

At the time of writing there were about 1900 permanent deacons in the Episcopal Church and eighty in the Anglican Church of Canada. About seventy dioceses have a diaconate programme.

Despite this greater flexibility in the North American churches, the Anglican Communion worldwide would still seem to be struggling with the concept of a restored, and permanent, diaconate. As with other denominations one of the difficulties is often the perceived threat this renewed order creates for the presbyteral ministers:[33] 'Clericalism ever seeks to protect the turf of the clergy, although in this instance it is the turf only of the highly clericalized and powerful presbyterate.'[34]

It seems unlikely to be immediate, but almost certain to be soon, that the Anglican Communion will formally re-establish the diaconate in the manner suggested in the ecumenical discussions.[35]

The Lutheran Church in Scandinavia

Deacons in the Church of Sweden are principally involved in the charitable and social work of the church. Their liturgical role is limited, although it varies from parish to parish. Throughout the twentieth century the church has increasingly clarified the diaconal role. In 1921 the first official orders for the ordination of deacons and deaconesses were received by the church although the service was described as 'installation to a call'. In 1942 the new service book introduced the term 'ordination' into the services for the deacon and the deaconess. By 1987 it was being emphasized in the ordination service that the diaconate is: 'With Christ as example, to be a sign of mercy to the congregation'.[36]

Deacons in Sweden usually work within parishes, but their work is extremely varied, including all forms of administration and social work. Most come into the diaconate already trained in either social work or nursing and receive their training in diaconal ministry afterwards.

Diaconal ministry in the Norwegian Lutheran Church is very similar to that in Sweden. The history is similar and the focus is on nursing and social work. The diaconal training college is a descendant of the old Deacons' House founded in 1893 and the present International Centre, with hospital and college, was established in 1987. The deacons and deaconesses are seen as lay and the college trains for secular, as well as church, employment. The emphasis is on diaconal ministry as a calling, however it is carried out.

Lutheran Churches in America

The variety of ministry amongst this wide group of churches makes it difficult to generalize. Deacons are not present in most of the churches, but the Hanover Report[37] is dedicated to 'Tom Dorris, a Deacon in the Evangelical Lutheran Church in America'. Whilst their tradition does not encourage the ministry of deacons as such, many of the Lutheran churches in America are involved in some form of diaconal work or another. A particularly interesting development is that of the 'Stephen Ministry'. Started over twenty years ago it has spread to over 4,600 congregations in North America, Great Britain and the Middle East. Stephen Ministers are trained to befriend in a confidential way. It is largely one-to-one, but is undoubtedly a development of a form of diaconal ministry.

A recent development in the Evangelical Lutheran Church in America is the proposal to enter into full communion with the Episcopal Church. Within the proposal it states that: 'the ELCA is not required by this proposal to ordain deacons or diaconal ministers.'[38] This decision would seem to close the door to any ordained diaconate. It will almost certainly create a period of confusion within the two churches as they attempt to grow closer together.

The Presbyterian Churches in Great Britain

Within the Presbyterian Churches two separate forms of diaconate have developed. Some congregations have maintained the Calvinist concept of a Deacons' court consisting of minister, elders and deacons. Such deacons were in fact the church managers and administrators. Within the Presbyterian churches the spiritual care of the congregation is entrusted to the elders. Several of the Presbyterian churches found themselves with deaconess orders in the later part of the Nineteenth century.

These deaconesses were involved in nursing care and pastoral work and, in more recent times, as assistants to ministers. The Church of Scotland was one of the earliest with Lady Grisell Bailie set apart as a deaconess in 1888. This new ministry spread rapidly to the Presbyterian Church in Ireland, to Australia and from there in 1900 to New Zealand. Yvonne Wilkie, the Archivist of the Presbyterian Church of New Zealand has commented that the order came about without conscious decision and that it did not gain its constitution until 1936. The Church of Scotland did not actually approve a deaconess scheme until 1962. The Church of Scotland still struggles with both practice and theology of the diaconate but has an active diaconate. This diaconate is not at present ordained, but this is part of the ongoing discussion.

The United Reformed Church

When the Congregational church and the Presbyterian church in England came together to form the United Reformed Church in 1972 the new union inherited the Deaconess Order of the Presbyterian Church. Diaconal ministry, as such, was considered to be something the new union would wish to preserve, but the Deaconess Order should cease to recruit. The last of the deaconesses, Kay Salvage, was commissioned in 1975 and in 1981 the first Church Related Community Worker came out of training. By 1998 there were ten CRCWs in post and the church had commissioned a Report on the work of the CRCWs as mission. This Report has recommended the expansion of the programme to thirty workers. This form of 'diaconal ministry' has something in common with the ventures in the Lutheran churches in the Nineteenth century.

That these workers should not be called deacons is the result of the differing traditions brought together within the United Reformed Church. The Congregational church had deacons who were similar to the elders in the Presbyterian Church, but who had a greater administrative role. At the time of union it was agreed that the term elders should be used and the role was brought into one. This change meant one partner giving up a cherished tradition and it would be insensitive to reintroduce this terminology for a quite different ministry. Another reason was that the deaconesses were ordained, but this ordination was not only ontologically different to that of presbyters, but different in intent. Deaconesses were ordained but considered lay, which relates more closely to the ordination of elders than to that of ministers of word and sacrament.

Some idea of the understanding which the URC has reached about this new mission venture can be gained by the following quotations from the section on theology in the Report:

> 'The main difficulty is in overcoming the separation between church and community.'
> 'One CRCW comments, 'As I don't work directly with the church I LISTEN to the community.''
> 'This depends upon the church being able to hear God's Good News from the community.[39]'

The Methodist Church in Great Britain

In 1986 the Methodist Conference invited candidates to the Wesley Deaconess Order, both men and women. It had been closed to recruitment since 1978 with the intention of forcing the Church to look at the Order seriously and consider its future. 'Since the 1960s, recruitment had been falling and those who did come into the work had not lasted long.'[40] The church started to look at a variety of ways of responding to this problem, including the possibility of setting up a Methodist Order of Mission and Ministry. This latter was to be an amalgamation of all the 'lay' workers in the service of the church and was seen as a new way forward. This proposal was soundly rejected by Conference in 1988 and the Wesley Deaconess Order was renamed the Methodist Diaconal Order. The Connexional office and the Order were then instructed to bring formal proposals to clarify this situation and have been engaged on this task for the last ten years.

Until 2000 recruitment to the new Order had been steady. Candidates had numbered from twenty-five to thirty-three each year of whom around ten-twelve have been accepted. The Order was growing at a pace roughly equal to the work available. Since the advent of Foundation Training[41] there has been an alarming slump in candidates.

Where and how deacons are trained has also changed. The deaconesses boasted their own college where the training was rigorous, both academically and in practical terms. Now deacons are trained alongside the presbyters in colleges and courses spread over the country. This means that the newer presbyters will have encountered deacons before they go into circuit, which will mean, not only a higher awareness for the Order, but also that almost all deacons undergo training identical to that of their colleagues training for the presbyteral ministry. The downside of this process is that while most Methodist deacons are now well-trained presbyteral ministers, their diaconal formation is difficult to discern.

Diaconal stationing differs from that of presbyters. Deacons are sent rather than invited, to a circuit. The appointment they are sent to is worked out by the circuit and agreed by the Order, who then attempt to match an available deacon to the work required. All members of the Order expect to have a measure of community work in their job specification, but this varies from circuit to circuit[42]. Although a growing number of circuits are asking for deacons to undertake a diaconal project, there are still many situations, probably the majority, where the membership see themselves as short of ministry (in the sense of being ministered to). In these latter cases the circuits vary greatly in their response to the situation, from those who simply want a token community involvement and a largely presbyteral role, to those who have worked out an innovative diaconal scheme.

One of the difficulties faced by circuit ministers, members, and deacons alike is the lack of real understanding of what diaconal ministry entails. In fact there has been a great difficulty in presenting a coherent image and clear interpretation of the role of the deacon. The process whereby Conference enacts legislation and then sends the legislation to committees to work out the detail has contributed to this. As mentioned earlier the decision to reopen the order was taken by Conference, which passed the establishing of guidelines to the Faith and Order Committee and the Methodist Council, who worked in parallel. The circuits have not yet been offered a clear and unambiguous understanding of diaconal ministry with which to work.

In 1988 the report to Conference The Ministry of the People of God stated:

> 'It may seem strange that in a report which emphasizes the point that all members of the body of Christ have a ministry we use the word 'minister' to refer exclusively to one who is ordained.'

Despite the fact that the Methodist Church had been ordaining deaconesses since union in 1932, this paragraph did not include them as ministers either. 'Minister' meant only 'presbyter' even if the church in the same report rejected the use of that term. Nor did CPD[43] which has always included several pages of definitions and interpretations, include a definition of the term deacon or lay until 1998. The 1998 edition of CPD includes the new definitions of deacon as, a person ordained to the office and ministry of deacon. Lay is defined as someone who is neither a minister nor a deacon. Perhaps indicating the confusion within

Methodism, 'minister' has not been redefined and the definition still reads 'a minister of the Methodist Church admitted into full connexion', ordination not being mentioned! This definition would tend to indicate that reception into full connexion[44] is still the important part in the process.

For the last ten years there have been 'discussions' at Convocation[45] about the role and standing of the deacon. Much of this has been carefully channelled and there has often been quite specific guidance. Unfortunately, good theology cannot start with a limitation on what you may think or say. The result is that too often the definition of a deacon's role is a negative. This was seen most clearly at an ordination service a few years ago, when the preacher, a notable Methodist minister with a claim to scholarship, faced the largest number of ordinands since the Order reopened and preached a sermon that went 'Presbyters do . . . deacons don't'. Each of his sermon points started by describing a facet of presbyteral ministry and then suggesting that deacons do not have that responsibility.

The main misunderstanding in the minds of congregations arises from the fact that deacons normally do not preside at Holy Communion. In some denominations, this would not be a particular problem, as they have some understanding of different orders of ministry. In Methodism, there is no such understanding, and often no willingness to understand that the deacon is quite content with the situation and in fact, in most cases, sought it. This difficulty arises particularly where a deacon is the principal pastoral carer to the congregation.

A simplified definition of the ministry of the deacon that would receive wide acceptance, would be: to enable the ministry of the church to the community to which it relates. There is a very strong emphasis on this aspect of the deacon's role within the power structures of the Order itself.

Such a ministry can fit in well with the idea of a messenger, or an ambassador -someone sent[46]. Unfortunately, in many cases, those who are sent are without real authority (the ambassador only has authority when presented with credentials), and often without any apparent expectation that they should carry the church with them. In such situations it is common for the church to view the work being done as the deacon's and as having no real connection to those sending him/her which suggests a lack of understanding of both the representational and ambassadorial role.

Variety and Growth

Within the varieties of church response to the growing evidence of a vocation to diaconal ministry, there are many parallels. Almost all churches would seem to have developed a view of the deacon, male or female, as a minister of God's charity. Many, from the Roman Catholic to the Church of Scotland, are beginning to develop an understanding of the deacon's role as 'representative'[47]:

> 'But it is a service, a *diakonia* in which deacons only *prompt* the people in their response of prayer and praise and do not act on their behalf, and in which they guide them in their service to mankind and do not undertake it for them [48]'

The history of diaconal ministry within the world-wide universal church has been diverse and multi-faceted. The early church has left us with little from which to re-create a standard model, but a mass of unravelling threads to pick at. Time does not seem to have knitted them neatly together. On the contrary, threads can be found in all sorts of places in every time, pointing in a multitude of directions. The constants are few, but they are there.

The first, and undoubtedly the most important, of these constants is that diaconal ministry is the expression of the charity of the church. In this it has always been intended to point to God's love and to be the visible, practical representation of the commandment to love your neighbour as yourself. It was in this sense that it began and that has been the official church definition at almost all stages of history.

Whenever the church has offered the deacon/deaconess a merely liturgical role, some form of diaconal ministry has emerged from within the body of the church. This has sometimes been led, or co-ordinated by, the ordained presbyteral ministry of the church, but has usually been inspired by informal activity and an offering of service from within the laity.

The second constant has been that diaconal ministry has been a ministry in which women have been active. Whilst women have only been a part of the ministry of word and sacrament in fairly recent times, this is not so in diaconal ministry. From the very earliest times there were female deacons. As the church became hierarchical, and the position of women in society affected their role in the church, gradually the term deaconess came into use and the women's role as 'deacon' was stripped of its authority leaving the deaconesses with the functions attached to propriety[49] at the baptismal services of the church. Once the ordained deacon was reduced to the probationary stage of the priest's training even this avenue of service was closed to women. Although women entered the religious orders, these were enclosed in the Middle Ages and offered little opportunity for diaconal service. A particular feature of the nineteenth century upsurge, which has led us to the present situation, began with women offering for service.

The Roman Catholic Church is the exception to the rule so far as women are concerned. The new and fast growing permanent diaconate is different from a deacon in the threefold ministry and there seem to be serious suggestions in many sectors of the Catholic Church that women should be allowed to enter the diaconate.

The third constant has been the official church response to an active and growing diaconate. As a separate (they would say complementary) ministry within the church it has become a focus for concern about roles. In the early church it was the growth of the diaconate, and its power as the active arm of the bishop, which threatened the presbyters. First deacons were made subordinate to presbyters and then, gradually, the role was absorbed into that of the presbyter. During the nineteenth century renewal of the diaconate it was principally a ministry for women. During this period women were subordinate to men in law and social standing, and so could not offer a threat to anyone's role. All of the new diaconates were administered by men, usually ordained ministers. As long as that remained the case the movement grew and flourished. The point of conflict seems to come at one of two points in the growth of a church's diaconate: either when the order admits men, or when it is given some form of autonomous authority.

In the Church of England, women as deaconesses were acceptable and seemed to create no difficulty for the church. Women as permanent deacons, alongside an all-male priesthood, were tolerable but a permanent diaconate, with both men and women, becomes a problem. There are few dioceses where the formation of a permanent diaconate is encouraged and for most deacons, male or female, the control is economic. Remaining a deacon usually means being non-stipendiary.

In this way the modern deacon has had a limited authority and this has held the possibility of conflict with the presbyters at arm's length. The difficulty for the deacon is that there is no longer a clear ambassadorial role for the deacon either. No longer representative of the bishop, the deacon does not carry that authority. The struggle has been, and for some still is, whose authority do they bring? Who sends them?

Within the Roman Catholic Church the question of who gives the deacons authority has become more clear as the statements in

Sacrum Diaconatus Ordinum become accepted into the everyday life of many dioceses. Deacons carry the authority of the church, not the bishop today, but the local church. Although they are ordained, and brought into action under the authority of the bishop, it is the local church which they are required to represent. Deacons are to be rooted in the community and relate to the church locally. Despite the more orthodox liturgical role suggested as the primary role by the statement of Pope John Paul to the Congregation for Clergy in 1997[50] 'This service should first of all take the form of helping the bishop and the priest', the development has been toward the community role which the Pope included as secondary. The signs of their authority are the clerical collar and the title of Reverend which marks them out from the community in which they serve. The clear sign of who has sent them is in their liturgical role and their ordination.

Within the Church of England permanent deacons are also marked with these signs of authority, but there is still a question as to whether their ordination is complete. The Church of England seems to have little idea of where or how to send them, it has not yet defined a role for deacons. It has 'recognized' calling in ordination but, with no recent tradition of a permanent diaconate to call on, is unsure how to proceed further.

It is important to understand one or two particular points revealed by this research. The first of these is that there are two quite separate strands of diaconal theology. One of these is an ordained, representative ministry in which the deacon is the focus for the image of the Servant Christ and in an ambassadorial role to be the church in the community beyond. The other, Reformed, strand offers a deacon who is lay and is commissioned to organize and do charitable work on behalf of the church. There are positive and negative things to be said about each system, but they are clearly rooted in different theological understandings, although they can be shown to have the same origin. What

Methodism has done and what it has said suggests that it is not sure which tradition it should claim.

The second point is that we should not overlook the reality of the traditions we claim. The role of the seven in Acts was to distribute the common wealth fairly amongst the membership of the community. The deacons in the early church took the gifts brought to the table and distributed them to the faithful needy. Luther's diaconal community was in the context of a Christian nation in which every household paid a tax to the church and this is still the context of diaconal work in Scandinavia. The very recent concept of sending community development workers out to those seen to be in need rather than trying to bring those in need into the church for care is a courageous development of the 'love your neighbour principle'. If it is to work it must be acknowledged for what it is and owned as a new thing.

Ordination in the Methodist Church of Great Britain - A Lack of Clarity

Despite a long tradition of ordination to diaconal ministry, dating at least from Methodist Union in 1935, the Methodist Church is ambiguous in the language it uses for this concept. The term 'ordained ministers' is applied solely to presbyteral ministers. Thus Trevor Rowe could write:

'In 1988, proposals were brought for a Methodist Diaconal Order, open to men as well as women and marked by three factors - *ordination*, lifelong commitment and availability for stationing, (indicating) a parallel with *the ordained ministry* from which it would be distinguished by being diaconal rather than presbyteral.[51]'

Such statements have a considerable history in Methodist writings. In 1966 Gordon Wakefield contributed an eight-page essay[52] to *Service in Christ*, a volume of essays on *diakonia* from a wide ranging theological and ecclesiological background. Within 'Diakonia in the Methodist Church Today' there is only half a page on the Wesley Deaconess Order. Wakefield describes the Order by quoting from the ordination service for deaconesses. Part of this quotation reads:

'It may fall to you to preach the gospel, to lead the worship of a congregation, to teach both young and old; you may be required to feed the flock of Christ, to nurse the sick, to care for the poor, to rescue the fallen. To succour the hopeless.[53]'

The author provides us with no comment on this quotation, but two pages later in discussing the role of the poor stewards[54] he goes on to say:

'If there were, in Methodism, a diaconate 'primarily concerned with ministering to Christ in the persons of the needy', would it not be appropriate to involve its members in the liturgy as assistants to the presiding minister, perhaps as distributors of the cup?[55]'

There has been considerable change since 1966, but the Methodist church still offers no liturgical role to the deacon and as can be seen from the 1997 quotation 'ordination' as applied to deacons has a degree of ambiguity.

In the recent reports to Conference the diaconate is said to be 'both an order of ministry and a religious order' but they are clearly not 'ministers'. Until 1997 deacons were treated as lay within the structures of the Methodist church and were eligible for all the lay offices at local church, circuit and connexional level but they were not eligible for ministerial offices. Since

1997 deacons are separated from the laity and the 'ministers'.[56] Deacons who preach do so as lay (local) preachers. Superintendent ministers tend to interpret this last status in different ways but to put emphasis on the 'lay preacher' status in some way.

All of this lack of clarity creates confusion, in the minds of the congregation, the presbyteral ministers and the deacons themselves. Some of the confusion has remained because of resistance to change. The reports have not always been accepted by Conference and the amendments introduced have added to the confusion.

PART THREE

CONGREGATIONAL RESPONSES AND
PERSONAL REFLECTIONS

Preface

A project that involved a number of people from the local church so intensely for two years and at a less intense level for a further year, which questioned and engaged with the congregations to this extent, ought to have brought about some change somewhere. This final section explains what the changes were and also considers what our discussions have to say to the church.

Nothing is simple, and if I had expected to reach this point with all my questions answered I would be disappointed. To some extent what we discovered raised as many questions as it answered, but these questions are better informed and start from a position that is learning to take account of reality.

Chapter Eight tells the local story, how the people who were directly involved in the project were affected by it and describes some of the conclusions to be drawn from the work. It is not the description of a situation vastly changed. The changes made were in people's understanding. That was useful and all of us were left better equipped to cope with creating and using a diaconal appointment. What this project could not change also became clear. The process through which diaconal appointments are arranged does not start locally, nor is it the congregation's understanding of ministry, diaconal or otherwise, that affects the design of such an appointment. The changes in understanding would have to be at Connexional level if they were to have an effect.

With the above in mind, Chapter Nine considers what has been learned that has a broader application and offers some thoughts about the way forward for the Methodist Church. I suggest that the present process hinders the best deployment of deacons and indicate what seem to me to be some of the weaknesses, while offering an alternative process which could bring about a more constructive use of the ministry of deacons, without some of the tensions of the present process.

Chapter Eight

The Project - What we learned

The project had sought to achieve change in two main areas. The first was to clarify the role of the deacon in Airedale and Townville Methodist churches. The second was to enable the two congregations to recognize and develop their own ministry to the local community.

It became clear that the process made different impressions on different people. The team was primarily involved in the process, being party to the planning of the delivery and taking a full part in the research that informed the project. Partly because teamwork engenders support, and partly because of the process of selection of the team members who would work together over such a period, the team were supportive of the project and its aims. Being part of the team gave them insights that worked on them in ways that could not be extended to the whole of the congregations.

The congregations received a great deal of information and changes took place in their understandings, not all of which, as will be shown below, were those intended. Perhaps the greatest change in understanding was in my own discernment of the deacon's role in the context in which I worked. Alongside this came the awareness that the role of the deacon, as deacon, can best be defined on a Connexional[1] basis. Locally the role is often set before the deacon arrives and is affected by the traditional expectations of circuits and congregations.

In the second area of enabling the congregation to recognize and fulfil their own ministry to the community, there was learning at all levels that brought both disappointments and understandings. Both the team and I had built up unrealistic expectations about what could be achieved. Given that our congregations were elderly and the younger minority very involved we had thought there were things they might do. The expectations that we built up were not great, but based on the assumption that people who were active within the church could add another activity in an organization outside the church. We failed to take into account that elderly people do things at home that they will not even attempt to do outside. For many people the church is a second home and they are safe there, doing things such as committee work and some pastoral caring amongst people they have known all their lives. Outside that environment they are, quite reasonably, not prepared to take risks.

Understanding the Role of the Deacon

Changes in the Team's Understanding

The team were party to the project and they had gone through the process collaboratively. Their starting point had been the view of my ministry which was revealed in the assessment forms and evaluation meetings early in the process. From these returns it was clear that the work pattern they imagined for me was largely church-centred. Yet there was an acceptance that I would spend time in the community.

Discussion of the role expected was always frank, and brought out some views which helped me to understand where they were coming from. Within the group there were those who felt that presiding at communion should be possible for anyone. There were some who started from the position that, as their pastor, this was simply another aspect of this role which they would have hoped that I could fulfil. Only Peter Wadsworth, who had been part of the circuit team who had set up the appointment, could see that this would lead to my ministry being indistinguishable from that of the presbyteral minister and therefore create the same expectations within the congregations.

At the end of the project the team and I tried to quantify changes in their attitude to, and understanding of, the role of the deacon. They all agreed that the deacon *should* serve more outside the church than within it. Mike Dixon said that he had come to understand and value the differences in the two forms of ministry (presbyteral and diaconal). Maureen Dean, who had been involved in the circuit discussion team and was our senior Circuit Steward, told us, 'The circuit hadn't any idea what it wanted a deacon to do. Roles have crystalized as time went on, things the circuit hadn't dreamed of.' The first part of Maureen's statement was perhaps the most important for the future, as the circuit now realized what was being done in their name, but were still not clear as to whether that was the deacon's role.

The team agreed that here was a good level of approval for the community work and it was clear that most of this role would be asked of a new deacon coming into the circuit. The need for the deacon to fulfil a pastoral role within the local church, and the level of involvement in leading worship, was still felt to be a requirement. It is unfortunate that the expectation that the deacon should be allowed to preside at Holy Communion still seemed to be important to them. These expectations would make it difficult to differentiate the role from that of presbyter and could therefore mean the continuing presence of the problem.

Changes in the congregations' understanding

A survey of the members[2] that had been conducted before the start of the project had asked four questions of the congregation. To the question 'Why do you think the church is here?' the most popular answer was 'to worship God'. In response to the second question, 'How often do you think your deacon should visit you?', almost everyone had responded with 'when in need' or 'when sick'. There was no indication of an expectation of regular visits. The third question offered eight options for the deacon's use of time and asked for these to be put in order of importance. Only twenty per cent of those responding placed 'work in the community' in the top two places. Overall the most important two functions were given as visiting members and funeral visits.

The fourth question required the respondents to answer in their own words and said: 'Deacons would claim to be a focus of the servant ministry of Christ for the Church. Whom do you think they should be serving?'. Although a majority indicated a desire for the deacon to have a greater involvement with the activities and the people of the church, there was a significant minority who included phrases such as 'wherever there is a need'. The responses suggested that no one knew where that need might lie, if not within the church.

On the 12th of October 1998 I gave a talk to a fellowship meeting attended by eighteen people, at which I explained some of the work I was doing within the community and how this work affected the time I could spend within the church family. At the end of the talk I handed out question sheets. The question on the sheet was:

'If you were on the committee planning a new diaconal appointment in this circuit what is the most important thing you would want the deacon to do?' Fifteen sheets were returned and of these nine placed commitment to the church as the most important, including statements such as 'preaching the gospel' and 'promote pastoral care'. Four responses suggested community work but added that the church work must not be forgotten. Only two seemed to suggest community work as a primary role.

In real terms nothing had changed in the congregations' view of the deacon's role. Their focus was still church-centred. Despite regularly applauding the results of work in the community, this work was not given a high priority as against work within the church and for the congregation.

In the summer of 1998, with the inclusion of a ninth church into the circuit, the circuit meeting decided that it had a case under the deprivation rules for an authorization for someone other than a presbyter to preside at Holy Communion.[3] It was the circuit's wish that I as deacon should be given this authorization. If I refused to accept this situation the circuit would have taken the option of having an authorization for a lay preacher. This solution would have hurt and upset the congregations at Airedale and Townville and, despite my beliefs about the deacon's role, I found it unacceptable to put myself in the position of standing aside while a lay person presided at Holy Communion in the churches in my care. Within the congregation there was a very positive response to my being granted an authorization to preside at Holy Communion. Quite a number of people came and told me how pleased they were and how nice it was that I could do this for them now. While this was personally very gratifying, it added to the evidence that the image the congregation had of the deacon remained unchanged.

Changes in my own understandings

Since I came to the project aware of the possible problems that could be created for the deacon by the congregations' expectations, I brought to the situation my own agenda.

My original job description, with its community emphasis and pastoral role within the churches, had seemed feasible and ideal for the practice of a diaconal ministry. What has become clear, as the situation has been examined and discussed with the team and the congregations, is that roles have a moulding effect. We are to some extent shaped by the roles that we carry out.

At the outset of the appointment the deacon's community role had not been defined. Its existence was clearly stated in outline, but there were no precise tasks. The pastoral care role for the two churches was more precisely delineated and all concerned had their own understandings of its boundaries. From the beginning it was easy to fulfil people's pastoral expectations. Quite quickly the congregations had put me into the mould of 'presbyter'.

In time I was able to develop my own community work, developing links with Homestart, the Drug Action Group and after eighteen months I had become involved in the Chrysalis Youth Project. As this process continued I found myself spending more time on the community work than on the pastoral care.

From the beginning of the appointment I kept careful records of my pastoral visiting, with the intention of being even-handed in the way that time was distributed between the two congregations. But the number of pastoral visits declined over time, the decline beginning at the point at which the community role began to establish itself in my ministry.

The congregations now had expectations, which I was not fulfilling. Subsequent attempts to strike a balance have proved unsuccessful. The initial stage had set the pattern and built the expectation. If that expectation was met then the community role must be limited. To create my vision of diaconal ministry it was important to take up the challenges presented by the community, and to try to bring the church into that situation with me. Like my predecessor I made choices. My choices have meant that the pastoral care of the congregations has suffered in comparison to the early period and they are aware of their loss.

The Congregations' Ministry

The intended change in enabling the congregations to recognize their ministry to the local community was a much more successful process. Speakers, talks and sermons all produced positive results. It was in the extension of this process beyond the immediate churches that an interesting and essential discovery was made.

Responses to the speakers and displays

The displays from the local community organizations were seen by all those who used the church during the week and by the Sunday congregations. They were related to the speaker's presentations and provided an ongoing opportunity for people to ask about the church's involvement with the organizations portrayed.

It was not possible to have the same group make-up for each of the speakers as the fellowship groups have a flexible membership. A core group would have heard all the speakers and all would have been present at more than one presentation.

Members of the team attended each of the speaking engagements and I questioned the chair of each meeting afterwards. The congregations were asked to fill in a questionnaire at the end of the series that offered a range of responses from 1-7, with 1 being the highest score. The questionnaires showed a good response to the speakers. Fifty per cent responding in the 1-2 range, twenty-eight per cent in the middle range (3-4) and only twenty-one per cent in the 5-7 response area. The responses in the 5-7 area all drew attention to the age of the congregation and gave this as their reason why they could not be expected to involve themselves in the organizations. The majority, who did not take this stance, nonetheless suggested that it was the deacon's task to be involved rather than the congregation's, but they were happy to support that involvement.

The deacon's talks

I gave talks to both of the fellowships which meet at Airedale and also to three fellowships in the wider circuit. These were intended to give a wider view of the involvement I have in community projects. I gave prominence to the youth training and development project (Chrysalis) which had occupied so much of my time over the two years of the project. Within the congregations at Airedale and Townville these were greeted with interest and even enthusiasm while also producing a concern that this work was occupying too much of my time. That the church should be involved with helping young people with employment and education problems found general approval amongst my listeners. At Airedale there was already a general understanding of some of the problems from which these young people suffer. Concern was expressed about drug abuse and how the project might address this problem. The ambivalence expressed in the questions about the extent of my time seemed to be a concern about their loss of ministry. The general trend of such comments suggested that the work with the community projects should be in addition to the pastoral work in the church. No one could instance any particular pastoral concern that had not been met. One of the congregation suggested that I did not visit the fellowships as often as my predecessor. This last was true, but seemed of small concern to most of the members.

When these talks were given to churches in the parts of the circuit for which I held no pastoral responsibility, the response was extremely positive. This response was particularly noticeable amongst people who had not been aware that this work was being done. They were then moved on to ownership of the work and appreciation that it was being done in their name.

Here again was a clue as to the source of the problem that we were attempting to tackle. In the churches in which the deacon was responsible for the pastoral care of the congregations, though there was approval in principle for the carrying out of this work, it was seen to be at their expense. In the churches where there was no pastoral responsibility there was not only a higher level of approval, but a desire to be better informed and to come into a more immediate ownership of this work.

Participation in the projects.

One of the hopes, which we had built into the project, was that people from the congregations would be encouraged to participate in, or at least observe, some of the activity of the various community projects to which I related.

This hope had a very limited success. The Probation Service food collection scheme was new, and a very good way for the church to be involved with the community work, but it was exceptional. Mike Dixon, who chaired the team meetings, became involved in the AIM meetings but because of difficulties with meeting times his attendance was intermittent.

In retrospect there was a degree of lack of realism in this expectation. Many of the congregation were intimidated by the suggestion that they should sit in on meetings at which they felt they might not feel competent to offer a contribution. However, there are a few members of the congregations who are still active and have an appropriate background for such a role. But, it is this group of people who are involved in the running of the church and in full-time employment, leaving them little time for further community involvement.

The Deacon's Ministry - Developments

What did we hope to do?

One of the problems we had identified was that the congregations knew little about the community involvement. Our discussion identified this as not only a practical problem but also a theological one. If the congregations did not know about my work in the community how could that be a representative presence? If there is no 'sender', the 'ambassador' can only act on his/her own authority.

The project helped communicate to the church about my work in the community. After speaking to one of the fellowship meetings about this work the chairperson, in her closing words, said:

> 'Without Ronnie's involvement as a deacon in the community, we would not have learned about the work of GASPED and the Probation Service in our community. These are important issues.'

I established a pattern of reporting to the church councils about some of the work and including elements of information about the projects in fellowship talks and prayer life. One member of the congregation at Townville commented:

'It is good to know and appreciate that we in our church have a good representative reaching out into the community, seeking out the needs which so often are overlooked.'

Progress in this way means that there was a far greater appreciation of the work that I was involved with in the community and everybody in the congregation gained some knowledge of some of the projects. There were a reasonable number of people in the congregations who were very well informed and a much greater sense of participation.

Unchangeable elements

At an early team meeting, the superintendent minister, John McCarthy commented that he felt that the demands of preaching, laid on the deacon, had got in the way of the vision for a diaconal appointment. During the first two quarters in the circuit (from August 1994), I was planned to preach eight times in each quarter.[4] By late 1995 this had increased to twelve times a quarter and by the time John McCarthy made his comment it had increased to eighteen. It remained at the eighteen to twenty mark for the remainder of my appointment in Castleford. There was no suggestion on the part of the team or the superintendent that this should be lessened, neither was there any similar suggestion throughout the project.

Many of these preaching appointments were in the two churches that were in my pastoral care and a considerable number of these had always included the special elements such as the church festivals and baptisms. Nothing in the project was able to change the highly visible image this creates in the eyes of the congregation, and in the response sheets there was an overall sense that people expected the deacon to fulfil the role of the presbyteral minister as they understood it. This did not change in any significant way throughout the project.

The authorization - and its effects

As has been noted previously,[5] the circuit requested Conference to grant an authorisation for me to preside at Holy Communion. Although this did not in fact come into effect until September 1999, some two months after the end of the project, the discussions and the circuit's decision took place during the period of the project. This, very public, change in my function had an ongoing effect on the result of the project. There was an almost visible relaxation in the congregation and a sense in which they were saying 'it doesn't matter what he says, he'll be a "proper minister" now.'

My subjective assessment of the effect it has had on me is that I am aware that there has been a reversal of the direction of struggle. In the past I struggled to provide a pastoral role in the church, while fulfilling the community role, as I understood it to be. After the granting of the dispensation I felt that I was struggling to maintain the community role while I was drawn into the sacramental and pastoral role of the presbyter.

What Has Been Learned?
Any response to this question would necessarily be layered. The project has had its effect at three different

levels; within my own understanding, at the team level, and within the congregation generally.

What have I Learned?

Through the study and the working out of the project I have been able to come to a greater understanding of the traditions, the theological roots of the diaconate, and how they are reflected in modern practice in the church catholic. Alongside this, there has been the response of the congregations with which I have worked, and the practical working out of some of this theology in a Methodist circuit.

My enhanced understandings concerning tradition and theology are reflected in the three research chapters. The project, which was shared with the team and the congregations, has helped me to understand the way the congregations receive their perceptions of the deacon's ministry. One of the things I have learned is that my understanding cannot be definitive. The deacon's ministry has always been mutable, and diaconal ministry too has to fit the context of the church from which it emanates.[6]

What has become clear is that a deacon, given the pastoral care of churches, can no more hope to fulfil a community role than can a presbyter in the same situation. The church at a local level has not only an expectation that the person in pastoral care of their church will minister to them, but also a very strong traditional pattern of how that ministry should be carried out. While all ministers bring their own variations, the core content cannot deviate too greatly or the church will begin to feel deprived, uncared for and react accordingly.

Despite this expectation, it seems that there is a real difference in the way this ministry is delivered. More importantly, ministry must be offered to the body before the body can offer ministry to the community. There are two biblical precedents that illustrate this. *If* the seven in

Acts were the models for the first deacons, this was why they were ordained. The Christian community lacked ministry and the Apostles were looking outward. In 1 John 14:19 it says 'we love because he first loved us.' A congregation that does not feel loved will find it difficult to offer love. A deacon, called to represent Christ who serves has a clear responsibility to enable the congregation to feel loved so that she/he can enable them to love.

The project also taught me the importance of ownership and belonging. Many people involved in the projects saw me as 'the church', but they clearly needed a particular relationship to make that concrete. For myself, I needed to belong, to be in relationship with the local church whose authority I wore.

What have the team learned?

Our research into the meanings of *diakonos* and deacon, and the way deacons had been used within the churches throughout history, constantly brought us back to the ambassadorial role. The deacon was sent to represent the sender, a person of authority and to act on their behalf. From the beginning of our local scheme, the assumption was made that the 'sender' in this situation was the two congregations. Our research revealed that this was not so and that, in a Methodist context, it is the circuit who sends the deacon. It is the circuit who employs, who decides the parameters under which a deacon will work and which is the prime authority for whom he/she acts.

Part of the problem we had encountered lies in the dynamics of a circuit. Often the vision will be that of one person, and that person is usually the superintendent. The authority to take the decision to bring a deacon into the circuit lies with the circuit meeting and everyone in the meeting will understand something different when 'minister to' and 'community' are spoken of. In such a situation an agreement will be reached, but not everyone will have the same understanding of what has been agreed. The day-to-day guidance a deacon receives will come from the superintendent, but the people whose expectations have to be fulfilled are the members of the circuit meeting. Methodist ministers (presbyteral or diaconal) would understand community as those to whom the local church relates, as in the use of the term 'Community Roll' to list people with whom the church has a connection, but who are not members of the congregation. The team's discussions with members of the circuit meeting indicated that they would largely understand community as the local church and its neighbours.

Ideally the deacon should work in partnership with a presbyter, whether this be in pastoral care of one or more churches over which the presbyter has charge, or working directly in tandem and sharing responsibilities according to focus.

What have the congregation learned?

The congregations at Airedale and Castleford gained a heightened awareness of the work with the community even though there has been little change in the perception that the congregation had of the deacon. He was still seen as a substitute presbyteral minister, as time passed and the role was fulfilled in a way that was more comfortable for them, it was less of a second best. There was undoubtedly a sense of pride amongst the congregation in the deacon[7] as 'their minister'.

As in other such situations it is not so much the reality that matters as the appearance. What the congregation need is someone who presents a high profile as their minister and who therefore carries out the functions traditionally attributed to that role. If there were a presbyteral minister fulfilling these functions the perception of the deacon would be different as these particular needs of the congregation would be satisfied. Until this is the case it will be impossible to change the congregations' image of the deacon.

Throughout my appointment there was support for the work undertaken in the community but it was always affected by what the members saw as their own needs. One member of the congregation stated in a response sheet, 'Our deacon has the care of two churches and their congregations and therefore the community work should not take up more than one third of his time.' Not only would that third be hard to quantify, but the two-thirds are often invisible. From my conversations with her I suspect that she would really want that third to be a third of my visible time rather than my total time. Service preparation, church administration, preparation of talks are all invisible work as was shown when the team attempted to quantify my use of time at the beginning of the project. The majority of pastoral work is, of necessity, invisible work also. The profile of the work in the community is raised, the more it begins to appear disproportionate to the local church people.

This 'Catch-22' situation has been part of the experience of presbyters for centuries and it would seem to be have its origins in the setting aside of the seven in Acts 6, for very similar reasons. If the congregation is to understand the diaconate it must be presented with a image which is discernibly different from that of the presbyter. The congregation needs both to understand how the deacon will minister to them, and to have agreed beforehand how the deacon will minister on their behalf.

Chapter Nine

Diaconal Ministry and the Future

A view towards the theology

One of the principal conclusions I have come to is that it is not the deacon's role to do *diakonia*, but to be the deacon. The purpose of this be-ing is to represent Christ the servant to the people and to enable them to undertake their personal *diakonia*.

A deacon is an agent of communication, a go-between in the service of Christ.

If we are absolutely clear as to who deacons are - the go-betweens of Christ - then we will not be caught in fruitless debates about what deacons are to do.[1]

In its outworking, this representation will always have to be a practical example as it is not possible to represent it in a purely abstract way. What this suggests is that the work that the deacon does is not necessarily something which members of the congregation need to take on board; it is an example. What the deacon does needs to be effective *diakonia* with a real purpose, but it also must be recognised as representative. A major purpose of this work is to provide an image of service to the church and to provide an image of the church to the community within which it is carried out. Thus, the deacon is a representative/ambassador of the church and a representative/image of Christ the Servant.

For such a representative role to be carried out successfully, it must be highly visible, and the church must be kept informed. Most importantly, the congregation must be helped to understand that it is being done on their behalf.

Diaconal Ministry

The Practice

Within the United Kingdom, the churches that have a diaconate at present have different ways of using this resource. This in turn creates different images of "deacon".

Within the Roman church deacons are almost always non-stipendiary and have a distinct, but not always accepted, liturgical role, and their servant role tends to be poorly understood. Deacons are called upon to represent Christ in their daily lives and do so visibly.

The Church of England is struggling with the role of permanent deacons. There is not, as yet, a clear understanding of what they are or what their role should be. Some are stipendiary, but most are non-stipendiary, and in general they have a very low profile, both within the church and in the world.

The Church of Scotland has a long established diaconate, with a clear servant role but virtually no liturgical role. Their deacons are few in number and many people within the Church of Scotland do not even know they exist. Even amongst those who do know of them, not all would be clear as to what their role in the church is, or should be.

Deacons in the Methodist Church still do not have a highly visible ministry and in many places their role is confused by their use as substitute presbyters. The Church, connexionally, does not as yet offer a completely clear image of diaconal ministry. Throughout Methodism the Order suffers from the same lack of awareness that is encountered within the Church of Scotland and elsewhere.

As can be seen from the above there are ways in which understandings of deacons in these denominations differ from each other. The role, fulfilling the servant ministry, seems to be agreed across the denominations, although the functions differ to some degree. The shared problems are those of lack of visibility and poorly understood definitions.

It should be noted that "deacon" is used for certain lay offices within some denominations. Baptist churches use the term for a local church officer, a lay person, who undertakes a variety of administrative and pastoral roles within that church. In Congregational churches it is the term for the group of lay people who govern the local church. These deacons would be locally ordained.

Lack of clarity

The clearest statement that I have encountered on the ministry of the deacon is that of the Roman Catholic Church:

'In every case it is important, however, that deacons fully exercise their ministry, in preaching, in the liturgy and in charity to the extent which circumstances permit. They should not be relegated to marginal duties, be made merely to act as substitutes, nor discharge duties normally entrusted to the non-ordained faithful. Only in this way will the true identity of permanent deacons as ministers of Christ become apparent and the impression avoided that deacons are simply lay people particularly involved in the life of the church.'[2]

The deacon is set apart for ministry either through ordination or consecration. There are arguments for both, but the Reformed churches, in the main, prefer the latter.[3] Ordination may be defined as "consecration to ministry". Since most Reformed churches consider deacons to be lay officers, ordination is not seen as appropriate. Consecration, defined as "setting aside for holy purposes", is used in the Reformed tradition to indicate an office which is not necessarily permanent. Both ceremonials would include the laying on of hands and the offering of prayers.

Both the Roman Catholic Church and the Church of England have, in recent writings, made clear that one of the principal signs of entering the diaconate is to offer a lifelong commitment to this office. This is most generally recognised by the sign of ordination and it is in this context that ordination is suggested as the preferred option in the Lutheran/Anglican talks.[4]

Ordination to the diaconate is still not clearly understood by the laity within the churches and this is compounded by the lack of clarity expressed in some of the statements about the diaconate produced by denominational bodies:

'In comparison with the ministry of the bishop and the priest, the ministry of the deacon has greater difficulty in gaining recognition for its identity. The former have been entrusted with certain special tasks which strengthen their identity. . . The diaconate has no corresponding exclusive right. . . it is clear, however, that much still remains to be done to achieve generally accepted clarity regarding the place and role of the diaconate in the context of the Church's ministry in modern society.'[5]

Despite the comparative late entry into the process of re-establishing a permanent diaconate, the Roman Catholic Church statement mentioned above is clear and understandable. More than that, it would make a reasonable statement for most of the churches which have a permanent diaconate at present. Certainly the Church of England in its conversations with the Lutheran World Federation uses words which would suggest that this form would fit in well with their theology:

> 'Deacons have no special powers or activities exclusively reserved to them. What is, however, distinctive is their call to be publicly accountable servants of the church who have a call to model, encourage, and coordinate *diakonia.* This is the particular call or vocation of the deacon that is not shared by all Christians.'[6]

The Lutheran Church, if it were to move towards the Swedish model[7], as is suggested in *The diaconate as Ecumenical Opportunity,* could find the Roman Catholic description a good starting point for a more general statement. Although the Methodist Church could have a problem with some of the language, it too would find the Roman Catholic statement a useful clarification of its present position.

Unfortunately, although the statement is clear, its implementation has not proven easy for the Roman Catholic establishment to deal with. The bishops were given authority to establish the diaconate within their own dioceses and the right to choose not to do so. This has meant that in some countries, such as America, the diaconate has spread widely, whereas countries such as Great Britain have moved more slowly. One of the problems in expanding the diaconate for the Roman

Catholic Church in this country is the way in which some parishes have taken steps to bring the laity into a more active role in the liturgy. Many parishes have established a wide variety of lay ministries including that of eucharistic minister. This development of lay ministry has left little room in some places for the re-formation of a permanent diaconate. It will need time and patience for both forms of ministry to be allowed to develop appropriately.

Present Difficulties in the Methodist Church

However the Methodist church wants to use its deacons, it should always remember that they are a focus for, and an image, of the church's *diakonia*.

The use of deacons as substitutes for presbyters does a disservice in two ways. First, it devalues the diaconal role, with the laity struggling to understand the difference in the two roles. Presbyteral substitution creates a confusion in their perceptions of deacons that is really only resolved in terms with which they are familiar i.e. the presbyteral ministry. The deacon is seen as a subclass of minister and he or she is then questioned as to qualifications, training or ability. Amongst the presbyters, alongside whom deacons find themselves working in this way, tensions are created. Some are resentful of those whom they see as backdoor presbyters. Others, probably the majority, simply do not understand diaconal ministry as a separate order, and fall between the two stools of treating the deacon as an equal in ministry and acting as some form of overseer.

Secondly, it creates a point of stress in the deacons' own ministry as they still desire to fulfil their diaconal calling and to demonstrate and encourage *diakonia*. Where the deacon is called upon to undertake the presbyter's role and function it is the representation of Christ at the table which comes to be seen as their most important ministerial role. Representing the footwashing Christ becomes difficult because of limitations of time and because the congregation, presented with a familiar and comfortable image, will be reluctant to accept a different perspective on ministry.

Present Difficulties in the Wider Church

This separation of roles and distinctiveness of ministry, allowing presbyters and deacons to complement each other in their mutual ministry, is something which should apply in whatever church setting the deacon is found. Despite the clarity of the Roman Catholic statement on this matter, there are still dioceses in this country which have no permanent deacons. In those dioceses where there are deacons, their role is not always made clear or valued as much as the words of the statement would suggest; this is aggravated by the image of permanent deacons as solely liturgical ministers. The problem, which is also encountered in other denominations, is one of priests feeling threatened in their own role because the introduction of deacons has not been implemented as a partnership.[8] The document Formation of Permanent Deacons offers a diocesan plan for the introduction of diaconal ministry that can help to obviate this problem.[9]

The situation in the Church of England is similar, but even less formalised. There has been no real conclusion to the discussions about a permanent diaconate. Some dioceses have been very active in promoting diaconal ministry, whilst others have made no progress whatsoever. At the same time priests see themselves as ordained to the diaconate and it is normal for them to carry out those remaining liturgical functions of the deacon such as bringing the prayers of the people or proclaiming the word where those functions are not already delegated to readers. As long as this is the situation it will be impossible to offer a representation of the servant ministry as an equally important part of the church's calling.

It cannot be the function of one person to act as focus for two things at the same time. Inevitably, the presbyter who attempts to do this must fail to satisfy in one role or the other. If the presbyter seeks to fulfil the role of the deacon, availability and accessibility become part of the time-consuming demands of receiving petitions, responding with charity, organizing and leading the charitable works of the church through the congregation. If the presbyter gives the primary focus to the ministry of Word and Sacrament, as the apostles did, then the ministry of charity, the *diakonia* of the church, is neglected. Of course what actually happens is that the congregation elects a lay deacon to fulfil the function. What is happening then is that the charitable function as a representation of the love of Christ is disappearing and we drift into welfare work. Herzog finds this an unsupportable situation. "Separated from *leitourgia, diakonia* would be the same as secular welfare work."[10]. That one can be good and not a Christian should be obvious; what does not always seem to be obvious is that doing good does not mean that you are a Christian. *Diakonia* has to be an expression of our worship.

The Church of Scotland uses its diaconate very much like the Church Army in the Church of England, as a lay Order. It is exceptional, though not unknown, for a deacon to have a liturgical role today. It is difficult to see how the diaconate of the Church of Scotland can be seen as "a representative ministry". It would be more accurately described as a specialist corps with limited functions. Theologically the Church of Scotland seems to lean towards the view that diaconal ministry is a part of the role of the elder. They may yet find themselves in the position of the United Reformed Church which, at its formation, applauded the diaconate as a gift from God, but could find no way to recognise it as "ministry".[11] The URC made the decision to replace deaconesses with church-related community workers as a means of delivering "social responsibility" work. In 1997 there were ten CRCWs for 1728 churches and in 1999 a decision was made to increase this number to thirty.[12]

Future Hopes for Methodism

The work done in the project points to a need for ministers, presbyteral and diaconal, to work together in a team, sharing the burden of ministry and doing so as equals.   In this way it would be easier to offer the congregations a picture of complementary ministries. To make this proposition work each must understand the appropriate responsibilities placed on the other, where these are shared and where these are peculiar to the relevant ministry. If this can be achieved in the circuits where there are deacons, it will begin to affect the view of people in circuits where there are no deacons and those in the connexional offices. Diaconal appointments are usually for five years after which they will often move on. The majority of these moves will be into circuits that have not had a deacon before. This mobility of deacons will help to make offer an experience that can, over time, spread throughout the Connexion.

Central to any process of change would have to be a more precise definition of presbyteral ministry and of diaconal ministry. Such a definition should not be overly prescriptive, but it must be clear as to the proper responsibility of each Order. We use the phrase the "ministry of the whole people of God" without seeming to take on board what that means. The ministry of which we speak is Christ's, and he demands that we all accept our part. Presbyters and deacons are to be understood as having particular callings, as do local preachers within Methodism.

It is the particularity of these callings which needs to be recognised and respected.

What this would mean in Methodist terms is that circuits approaching "the Order" for the stationing of a deacon should not look at how a deacon could fill a gap in their provision. They should consider instead how a deacon could add to their provision and how this would affect the ministers at present in the circuit.

Part of the problem for the Methodist Church in general, and the Methodist Diaconal Order in particular, is the very looseness of the language they have used to express what they mean by diaconal ministry. There seems to be an unwillingness to be too sharply definitive in case this should exclude someone else's stance. Laudable as such an aim is, it leaves it open for each person to interpret diaconal ministry for himself or herself. More dangerously, it allows the negative statements, which are much sharper, to become the defining norms[13]. The Roman Catholic definition offers a much more positive starting point, placing within the explanatory text some of the prohibitions which the Methodist Diaconal Order accept at present.[14]

The experience gained in the Castleford project indicates that, to be effective, deacons must be identified as both representatives of the local church and as having clearly delineated roles within the church. It would help this to happen if a statement were available which took The Permanent Diaconate as a model.

The present situation, which encourages the constant redefining of the diaconate by individual superintendent ministers rather than the church Connexionally, is seldom helpful and offers deacons little help in defining their own ministry. It is a situation which, owing to a lack of clear parameters, usually starts from negative assumptions. There are occasions when superintendents ask their circuits to design a special appointment for a deacon, often when the circuit is losing a presbyteral minister. In the absence of clear guidelines the presbyters involved tend, naturally, to start from the position of "what things are my responsibility?". This statement of their "area of responsibility" becomes the starting point for discussions as to what might be the work of the deacon. A more helpful starting point would be to consider how the addition of a deacon could bring about a more creative use of all the circuit's ministers.

A Theology for the Future

A Visible Representative

Donald Coggan tells of a visit to the house of a bishop in America. He was taken to the basement, now the bishop's chapel:

'In the middle of the room was the table, where the Eucharist was celebrated, a dramatic setting forth of the gospel through the elements of the bread and the wine. But — and this I had never seen anywhere before — underneath that table, on the floor of the chapel, stood a basin and a jug and a towel. That was all. But it was everything. It spoke to me that morning as no spoken word could have done. 'So *that* is what it is all about. *That* is what the Servant-Son did immediately before he went out to his death — "He took off his outer garment and, taking a towel, tied it round him. Then he poured water into a basin . . ." And *that* is what the church is all about 'I have set you an example: you are to do as I have done for you.'[15]

Here Christ *the* representative[16] is "representing" the servant to us, offering an example of discipleship for all to follow. It is in this way that the deacon too has to act in an exemplary manner[17]. The church has not taken the footwashing to be the institution of a sacrament, nor a command to repeat the action. We usually understand this as an exemplary act and it is as such that it has been used in the centuries since.

Many Methodist deacons would object to the suggestion that their ministry should be highly visible. The accepted ethos is that we are servants who should, in humility[18], not seek recognition: "be careful not to parade your good deeds before men to attract their notice"[19]. In the exercise of our representative ministry there is a dichotomy between this ethos and our call to *represent* the servant.

In an age when individualism is very much at the centre of society's ethos, we have to beware that we do not confuse our personal *diakonia* with our representative calling. In the Sermon on the Mount Jesus says "In the same way your light must shine in the sight of men, so that seeing your good works, they may give praise to your Father in heaven."[20]. Deacons need to differentiate between their personal good deeds and the things they do as representatives of the church.   The latter need to be recognised as part of the church's proclamation.

A Limited Resource

Deacons are comparatively few in number and are not present in every circuit or parish. All of the denominations, in which the diaconate has been revitalised, will need to recognise this and find a way to make this limited resource visible within the whole church. I am convinced that it is more important that the diaconate is visible *to the church* than to the community at large if they are to fulfil their representative function.

The diaconal role should primarily offer an example of service which applies to the whole church. It is not necessary that deacons should "do", but that they should enable the church to "do". Deacons encourage this by their presence and possibly through their persons:

> 'In terms of New Testament theology, "the ordained ministry" is, wrote Bishop John Robinson, "representative, not vicarious. It does not stand over against the laity, mediating between them and God, *and doing what they cannot.* It is commissioned . . . *To do in the name of the whole what in principle all can do.*"[21]

What the deacon does personally has to be seen as representative in this way and thus it should be "a light that shines before the world". Any such activity is not the personal almsgiving of the deacon to be done in secret. Hiding their light under a bushel is theologically unsound, yet in most denominations that is exactly what happens with deacons and their work.

Within the Castleford circuit the project brought a raised awareness of the work of the deacon, but this is not the norm. In many circuits the work the deacon does in the community is not recognised. There are still many Methodists who do not even know that there is a diaconal order within their church. If the work being done by members of the Methodist Diaconal Order is to be an example to the church then it needs to be visible and to be so beyond the immediate area of effect. There is a similar problem within the Anglican and Roman Catholic Churches. Many of the Anglican clergy I meet have never met a permanent deacon. Conversations with Roman Catholic priests have not shown any real understanding of their diaconate either. Often the Roman Catholic priest has seen them as unnecessary liturgical ministers who would re-clericalise some of the work now undertaken by the laity.

An Example of Service

The gospel writings point to the importance of service in the Christian life and this would seem to suggest that the Church must actively represent this requirement in a way which is not seen as beyond the reach of all Christians, ordained and lay. This would seem to be the proper role for the diaconate.

The limited resources of the modern church mean that it is unlikely that each parish, or circuit, will be able to have a deacon within it. Those denominations that have a permanent diaconate at the moment are frequently not in a position to afford this extension of full-time ministry. Even the costs of training such a number would make it an unlikely development.

Different churches have approached the problem in different ways. I would suggest that the principal need is not for high numbers, but for a highly visible diaconate, representing the servant ministry in such a way that the church and the world can understand the message.

As has been said in Chapter Four, the use of the word *diakoneo* in the mouth of Jesus, as quoted in the synoptic Gospels, presents a much more menial role than the use of the related terms within the other New Testament writings. This emphasis on a servant ministry is given great importance in the gospels and is reflected in the life of Jesus as we have it reported. Service is seen as the duty and ministry of all who follow Jesus. Clearly the *diakonia* to which Jesus calls his disciples is one of serving others, as in Matt 25:45, "He will reply, 'I tell you the truth, whatever you did not do for one of the least of these, you did not do for me.' "

The early church kept this idea of service alongside the presbyteral ministry by having the deacon serve at the Eucharist. When the presbyter took on both roles, the image that this intended to represent to the church was a unified one of Christ as priest and servant. From early times the priestly role has carried authority and power and was functionally about things which lay people may not do. This "specialness" of the sacramental ministerial functions creates a "specialness" around all the ministerial functions of the sacramental minister, creating a problem as to how to offer the one part of that ministry as an exemplary model.

Whatever some modern ministers may wish, they are primarily seen as representing that priestly function and this makes it difficult to provide an image of Christ *diakonos* also. In Chapter Eight we saw how complicated it is for deacons to fulfil the servant role the church has apparently asked of them, if they are also given the specific functions normally carried out by the presbyter.

It seems everyone accepts the value of *diakonia* as a part of the ministry of the church but that it is seen as "everybody's ministry". There is a sense in which things which are everybody's can become nobody's. When this sense of "everybody's" takes on the anonymity of "their's" ownership has been lost. Each member of the church has to be helped to understand that they have a personal *diakonia* to fulfil, and encouraged to find it. The deacon's task is to represent Christ, in person, as servant, both in the liturgy and the ministry of the church.

Insights for the Methodist Diaconal Order

Throughout its existence the Wesley Deaconess Order was administered by a male warden, always a presbyteral minister, and usually one of considerable authority in the church. This had advantages, but some disadvantages have only become of real significance since this ceased to be so.

After the Wesley Deaconess Order was reopened and became the Methodist Diaconal Order, it moved to having a warden who was a deacon. Although this should have been a good thing, it created a vacuum of authority for a time.

Throughout the period of redevelopment those who led the Order had come from a tradition of subordination. The new Wardens and senior deaconesses were used to working under authority and accepted the authority of the connexional committees as proper. On the connexional side the authority was being provided by committees, few of the members of which were familiar with the Order. The process of renewal began to be buffeted about, from opinion to prejudice and back again:

'If the answer does not come from our own story it will come from somewhere else. If it comes from somewhere else, the renewal of the Diaconate is doomed. Really. Besides, if you don't have a picture of what Diaconate is that is clear enough to allow you to say "no" without guilt, you are forever owned by other people's images of what a Deacon is supposed to be and do.'[22]

This has been part of the problem for the Methodist Diaconal Order over the past few years. The long tradition of service under authority has caused it to allow the ideas of others to dominate the process. Although all members have been part of that process, it has created tensions and struggles for many. Jim Liggett's prophecy may go too far, but it does contain a message for the Order. We must describe ourselves, create our own image, be confident in who we are. Then we will come to the circuits offering a vision we can own and no longer need to be described by others. Deacons will then be in a position to negotiate with circuits about their role in the ministry of the local church, rather than allowing the superintendent to create his or her own idea of a deacon.

The Methodist Church has described the diaconate as a full and equal order of ministry with the presbyterate, but in practice the diaconate occupies a subordinate role. Some of the ways in which this can be seen seem petty. Deacons have been ordained persons since Methodist union, but the church in its official documents and statements speaks of presbyters as *the ordained ministry*. We have previously noted that until 1997 deacons were ordained but remained lay, and although that status has changed, it is still not quite clear what the Methodist Church means by "ordained" when it speaks of deacons.

Discussion and communication about the stationing of deacons often appear to be restricted to a dialogue between the MDO and the superintendent minister. It is commonly understood that these discussions are a result of internal discussion at circuit level and these certainly take place, but the process is led, and often envisioned, by the superintendent. This process gives ownership to the superintendent, not to the circuit. Once in station, if things are to be changed, they are normally done at the superintendent's behest and sometimes with little discussion at circuit level. While deacons often have some freedom of interpretation, I have encountered no situations in which they have redefined their station to fit the circumstances as they have seen them.

Those called to diaconal ministry must be assumed to have some vision of it. Therefore, it should be through discussion amongst deacons that the vision can be best refined and defined. This is not a process separated from the church, but informing the church's thinking. The Methodist Diaconal Order must then have the courage, and the determination, to share this vision with the whole church.

If the limited number of deacons in the church are truly to represent the servant ministry of Christ, to be an example to the Church and on behalf of the Church, then they need to have a sharp focus, rather than the diffuse understandings of a wide variety of individuals. This sharp focus can only come about if circuits, who have been encouraged to have a deacon, have discussions with the Order in the same way that the presbyteral stations are set up, that is through the circuit stewards. The relationship created would help the circuit own and understand diaconal ministry. Subsequent amendments to fit the situation out of experience would be between the deacon and the circuit stewards and circuit meeting. This is not about where power rests, but where the vision lies. Such a system is not about giving deacons "rights", but using deacons appropriately. Moving the point of vision from superintendent to circuit stewards or circuit meeting will not be easy. Superintendents have not, as a body, appropriated this role so much as had it thrust upon them. If deacons are to empower the laity it has to start from a relational basis.

The Order needs to take on board the understandings about the interpretation of *diakonia* and *diakonos* as "ambassador" and "messenger". They should not be constantly amending the message they bear to suit the expectations of others. This ambassadorial role is not carried out on behalf of the presbyter nor even the local church but is carried out as ambassador of Christ, and the church, and should be defined with this relationship in mind.

Until we return to this representative position, we will continue to be seen as servants of individuals rather than of the Church, assisting the service of others rather than representing the service of Christ. The ecumenical role discussed in the next section cannot be carried out by those seen as assistants to presbyters, but it can quite clearly be a normative role for those who see themselves, and are seen by others, as ambassadors.

An Ecumenical Hope

The diaconal orders of each of the British churches are represented in Diakonia International, which includes Roman Catholics as observers. This is a loose organisation of the diaconates of churches from around the world. It is not a pressure group, but offers opportunities for diaconal ministers, from all the different traditions, to meet together and to discuss mutual concerns. It is seen as a meeting of equals and the organisation is always seeking points of convergence, rather than examining points of difference, in their denominational understandings. This growing acceptance of each other's diaconal ministry is becoming recognised as an important movement in the ecumenical discussions of many churches. Within the Anglican/Lutheran discussions this growing congruence has been directly recognised and in the conclusion to The Hanover Report[23] it is stated:

'The question and opportunity thus become clear: could forms of joint, common, or united diaconal ministry precede and clear the way for a joint, common, or united presbyterate or episcopacy? Joint oversight of diaconal ministries could provide a focus for movement into a joint exercise of *episcopé*. Our churches and our diaconal ministers need to be imaginative in shaping diaconal ministries ecumenically.'

What is being recognised here is the difficulty that has been encountered in the mutual recognition of ministries between the denominations. This problem often revolves around the different understanding of the Eucharist and the question of authority to preside. Despite efforts on the part of many, to come to some common understanding this has, as yet, not proved possible.

The diaconate, however, lies outside the Eucharistic problem and as such may offer a means of convergence between the different church traditions. If the diaconates can continue in their process of working together, it should be possible to reach a common understanding and to accept a common statement as to what a deacon is.

Such a result would offer real hope that the denominations would be able to recognise each other's diaconal orders and, ultimately, their ordination. What will be necessary is an acceptance of the flexibility in the models of ministry recognised, allowing each church to use deacons in their traditional way while coming to a common understanding of boundaries and functions. There are those who look for a common training and ordination for all deacons. It would be foolish to imagine that they will have their dream come true in the immediate future, yet there are Anglican, Methodist and URC presbyteral ministers, along with Methodist and Anglican deacons, training together already. There seems little reason why all deacons should not do the bulk of their training alongside one another. There may still be questions of denominational traditions, and perhaps some doctrinal understandings which would need to be dealt with separately, but that should be a small difficulty to overcome if the will is there.

The advantages of a common recognition of ministry are huge from the point of view of church unity and any step towards the mutual recognition of even one order of ministry is worth pursuing.

In Conclusion

The process of the study pointed us to what we discerned as "the problem" and helped to establish what created it. My research explored a tradition and theological base upon which to build a view of a modern diaconate, and the project helped to work out some of the ideas that I had thought could be applied.

That "the Methodist congregations of Airedale and Townville, who are without a presbyteral minister, are unclear about the role of the deacon in the church and in the local community" is a problem not likely to be solvable within the situation as faced. What became clear as the project progressed was that the problem was created beyond the circuit. The changes that are needed must take place at a connexional level and the cause of the problem addressed at the time of stationing.

A more helpful way to approach the deacon's appointment will be by providing clear definitions and boundaries so that the deacon can work from a firm base rather than a constantly changing position. Like a walker in a wild land it is important to keep the landmarks in line. It means looking over your shoulder at the tradition to see that you have not wandered too far away and lining up the future hopes so that the diaconate does not become either trapped in the past or aimless in the present.

Diaconal ministry is now firmly embedded in the Methodist Churches, well established within the Roman Catholic Church and has left the launch pad in the Church of England. Its growing theological coherence offers the denominations a bright hope for renewal in the twenty-first century.

It would seem that God is calling a growing number of people to offer for this ministry and that the churches are recognising this call, if not yet in a totally coherent way. What is not yet clear is why this is happening. In trying to respond to the problem presented in Airedale and Townville we have asked the question "What is a deacon?". The corollary is "what does God want us to do with these deacons?".

The upsurge of diaconal ministry in the nineteenth century was largely brought about by the vision of individual men who inspired others and brought them together in the new orders. Today the pressure comes from women and men who are responding, to what they understand as a call from God, to take up this form of ministry. The denominations are struggling, with the inertia of large institutions, to incorporate this vision into their thinking and activity.

For me the most important insight is the "plasticity" of diaconal ministry. We started by searching for a definition, a description of the functions of a deacon, or a key word, or phrase, which would make *diakonia* clear today. We found variety, change, a constant contextual realignment. Graham Cook, a URC Provincial Moderator, recently said that he understood presbyteral ministry by its functions.[24] Not everyone would agree with him, but it is clear that diaconal ministry cannot be understood by its functions; it is not a functional ministry. Deacons have "no exclusive rights"[25], "no special powers or activities reserved to them"[26]. By the nature of their calling deacons can fit themselves to whatever service is required by the church.

Fitting the service will always bring struggle and pain but this is inevitable if the deacon is to be part of a constant rebirth process redesigning him/herself to fit a new situation at every move. If the church and the deacons come to understand that the deacons' role is dictated by the service required of them by the situation into which they are sent the lack of clarity will cease to be a problem.

I have encountered deacons fulfilling many different roles: leading major projects, creating church on churchless estates, chaplains to many situations, parish workers, nursing orders, and even, in New Zealand, an Archdeacon in the Anglican Church in Wellington who was not an ordained priest. In the diaconate the church does not have a square peg struggling to fit a round hole, nor even a square peg comfortably in a square hole. It has a mutable peg that can fit almost any hole that needs to be filled, but it does not belong in any particular hole.

The question that a circuit should be asking when requesting a deacon is "What is our need?". The question for the deacon would then be "How can I respond to this need?". In this way what the deacon will offer will be a response to the need identified by the circuit and lead to a much more satisfactory situation for both parties.

NOTES

Chapter One

1 The Chrysalis Youth Project is a charity set up by a church and community group, sponsored by Airedale Methodist Church, to work with the young people of the estate. At the time of writing it was preparing to start on the building of a million-pound training centre on the estate.

2 Figures taken from a survey of the estate, The Airedale Project, for Wakefield Community Health Care by Cornelia Loosens, 1994

3 Intravenous Drug use and Health Related Issues prepared for Wakefield Healthcare in 1995 by Heather Fish, a researcher from Leeds University.

4 Report in the local newspaper on the opening. The cutting is in the safe at Townville but there is no newspaper heading to identify the paper.

5 A brief description from The Constitutional Practice and Discipline of the Methodist Church Volume 2, 1999 (Peterborough: Methodist Publishing House, 1999) may be of help to those not familiar with the MDO.

Standing Order 850 reads: (1) The Methodist Diaconal Order is a religious order to which those who belong to the order of deacon in the Church of God are admitted by the act of the Conference.

(2) The members of the Order offer lifelong commitment to diaconal ministry and a willingness to serve where the Conference directs. They exercise, alongside others, a pastoral, evangelistic and outreach ministry which reflects the servant ministry of Christ and enables the mission and service of the Church in the world.

(3) The Order shall have a Rule of Life, approved by the Conference, so as to provide a framework for the devotional life of each member, for discipline, mutual care and accountability, and for individual and collective commitment to the ministry of a deacon.

6 Methodist Council Diaconate Report, presented to the Methodist Conference, 1997.

7 Convocation is the annual gathering of the Methodist Diaconal Order, who are otherwise a dispersed community.

8 See page ?.

9 In some of the early church writings the deacon is called the Levite and whilst that terminology is no longer used, there is not only a possible similarity in role, the Levite is thought to have prepared the bread and mixed the wine and water for the high priest, but also a similarity of fate. In the earliest biblical writings God gave the people a special class of person to assist in their worship. By the time modern researchers such as Henry Gwatkin came to examine that role in the Judaism of the first century they could only find a porter and tender of animals.

10 Conference is the annual decision making body of the Methodist Church and its ruling authority.

Chapter Two

1 See page ?? re Jeannette Woodward.

2 At one early meeting, when people had been paired up and asked to find a reading that they thought had some relevance to servant ministry, there was a clamour for more guidance, in particular from the local preacher and minister. Edna silenced them all, by breaking into the requests for help and saying 'I'll read Romans 12'.

3 The Brigade factor, however, is still at work with three new church members from within the Girls' Brigade in 1994 and four new church members from the Boys' Brigade in 1998

4 The 1972 Circuit Report tells of the loss of two churches and a reduction to three ministers, 'the smallest number of Methodist ministers in the area for over a century.'

5 The Methodist church reserves the term 'minister' for ministers of word and sacrament. The Methodist Diaconal Order is an acknowledged order of ministry alongside the presbyteral order. For purposes of clarity I will use the terms presbyter and presbyteral where I am contrasting the two ministries.

6 Glenda Sidding was obliged to leave Castleford as a result of offering for presbyteral ministry, but was unfortunately unsuccessful in her candidature. Having turned her down for presbyteral ministry the church then stationed her as a deacon in a circuit which had suddenly lost a presbyter. She was given pastoral charge of the section

and granted an authorisation to preside at Holy Communion. She was to continue in this situation for seven years.

7 *The Ordination of Deacons and Deaconesses* (Peterborough: Methodist Publishing House, 1996).

8 Kevin Flynn, 'Once a Deacon' *Anglican Orders and Ordinations: Essays & Reports from the Interim conference at Jarvenpää, Finland, of the International Anglican Liturgical Consultation, 4–9/8/97,* (ed.) David Holeton Cambridge: Grove Books Limited, 1997.

Chapter Three

1 See W. H. Vanstone, *Love's Endeavour, Love's Expense* London: Darton, Longman and Todd, 1977 pp. 6–7.

2 There is only a short period in the life of the church in the west when diakonia would have been used to actually describe the ministry of the deacon. It would no longer have been used once the church became ∟atinised and a parallel language would have come into use. Calvin and the later reformers used the term when looking for a historical basis for the office of deacon and the Nineteenth-century founders of diaconal orders began to apply a narrower understanding of 'service' than the original application would seem to indicate.

3 At the time I left the circuit we had appointed a full time project manager. The building work on the project was starting and the funding stood at £1.2 million.

4 These figures are averages of the total times over the three weeks. The logged times were those which were clearly part of my working role and were spread over the waking hours.

5 Such as Mary Anne Coate, Trevor Rowe, Nell Rowley and myself

Chapter Four

1 See Chapter Three pp. 30-31

2 See Chapter Three, p. 31.

3 *Flying Leaves*

4 Paulos Mar Gregorios, *The Meaning and Nature of Diakonia*, Geneva. WCC Publications, 1988, p. 4.

5 Gerard Hughes *Oh God, Why?*, Oxford: The Bible Reading Fellowship, 1993, p 1.10.

6 See Chapter Five.

7 Richard Dillon in *The New Jerome Biblical Commentary*; T. F. Torrance,

'The Eldership in the Reformed Church', *Scottish Journal of Theology   34, No 4*: Anthony Bash, 'Deacons and Diaconal Ministry',

8 Ignatius of Antioch, *The Epistle to the Magnesians*, Phoenix. The Saint

Pachomius Orthodox Library Translated by Charles H. Hoole, 1885.

9 See Chapter Seven p. 80.

10 United Methodist Church, *The 1996 Book of Discipline*, para 319.

11 See 'the four necessary conditions of an authentic Diakonia' on page 36 above.

12 'willingness to identify with the served to the point of laying down one's life for their sake'.

13 John Collins *Diakonia*, p. 169 and 173.

14 The Methodist system of stationing presbyteral ministers by invitation is interactive, with the ministers seeking a circuit that fits their own needs. Although Conference is the ultimate stationing authority its function is largely to approve arrangements made. While mandatory stationing does occur, it is not the expectation of most presbyteral ministers at this time.

15 Barry Rogerson asked a similar question in his study of the diaconate: 'To whom does the deacon belong, or whose 'agent', 'go-between' or 'messenger', is he or she to be? Barry Rogerson, 'The diaconate: Taking the ecumenical opportunity?' in *Community - Unity - Communion: Essays in Honour of Mary Tanner* (ed.) Colin Podmore London. Church House Publishing, 1998, p. 213.

16 Gerald Arbuckle *Religious Life*

17 David Mullan, *Diakonia and the Moa,* Auckland, New Zealand: Methodist Theological College, 1984, p. 27

18 Conference, through the stationing committee, stations Methodist ministers in circuits. The process is one of consultation and consent, but Conference has the authority to send a minister where it will. Itinerancy was one of the original principal differences between local preachers and preachers in 'full connexion' who were then ordained.

19 It is the primary part of their role and calling to represent Christ the Servant to both the congregation and the wider community.

20 Chapter Five p. 62

21 See Chapter Five p. 62

22 For the deacon to claim an ambassadorial role on behalf of the community may be problematic, but the instruction in the ordination service 'interpret the needs of the community to the church' can suggest this role. Nevertheless there is a difficulty concerning whose authority the ambassador would act upon.

23 David Mullan, *Diakonia and the Moa,* p. 70 (the italics are mine)

24 It was decided at the Conference of 1997 that the terminology should be deacon as this was a non-gender specific term.

25 Extract from a letter from the Rev. John McCarthy, circuit superintendent, to the Rev. Donald English, General Secretary, Home Missions, 13th January, 1989. (The italics are mine.)

26 K. J. Payne, Superintendent, Castleford Circuit Report 1972

27 See Page 49.

28 Each presbyteral minister in a circuit has charge of a number of churches which are usually described as his/her section.

29 See letter on page 46.

30 Extract from the application form for a continuing diaconal appointment in the Castleford circuit, 15th July, 1993.

31 United Methodist Church, 'The Ordained Deacon in Full Connexion'. *The 1996 Book of Discipline,* paragraph 319 (Internet address http://www.umc.org/gbhem/319320 html, accessed 30/3/98).

32 GASPED is a rather awkward acronym for Group Active Support for

Parents Experiencing Drug problems.

33 A Methodist circuit consists of a group of churches ministered to by a team of ministers. It is customary for each minister to have pastoral charge of a section. In Castleford the Superintendent has three churches, with the largest, Trinity, being in the town centre. The second minister had three churches (recently increased by a fourth) with the largest being in Kippax. The deacon has had pastoral care of two churches under the charge of the superintendent

Chapter Five

1 John Calvin, *Institutes of the Christian Religion*, translated by Henry Beveridge, London: James Clarke, 1956, Vol. One, pp. 324-6.

2 *Strong's Concordance*. Hiawatha, Iowa: Parsons Technology, 1994.

3 John Collins, *Diakonia* offers an in-depth discussion of these words.

4 John Collins in his wide-ranging examination of the root words (of what he refers to as the diak words) has followed through a number of other words using the diak prefix to widen his net of source material. The words used in the context in which we are interested are only those above and I do not propose to consider any of the others which do not bear directly on the formation of the ideas about deacons and deaconing.

5 Collins, *Diakonia*: p. 77-95

6 W. H. Beyer in *Theological Dictionary of the New Testament*, (ed.) Gerhard Kittel, trans. Geoffrey W. Bromiley, Grand Rapids, Eerdmans: 1964.

7 Karl Barth, *Church Dogmatics, IV Part Three*. Translated by G. W. Bromiley,

Edinburgh: T.&T. Clark, 1962, p. 890.

8 C. S. C. Williams *A Commentary on the Acts of the Apostles*; Matthew Hengel *Acts and the History of Earliest Christianity* . Although Craig C. Hill 'Acts 6.1-8.4 division or diversity?' *History, Literature and Society in the Book of Acts*, (ed.) Ben Witherington III Cambridge University Press, 1996 contends that the whole Hellenist issue is based on a misunderstanding first introduced by F. C. Baur in 1873.

9 Canons of Neocaesarea quoted in *A New Eusebius*, (ed.) J. Stevenson, New edition London: SPCK, 1987, p. 293.

10 T. F. Torrance, *The Eldership in the Reformed Church*, Edinburgh: The Handsel Press, 1984, p. 13.

11 *The Epistle of St Ignatius of Antioch to the Trallians*, Translated Charles H. Hoole 1985   (http://www.ocf.org/OrthodoxPage/reading/St.Pachomius/Greek/ignatius.trallians.html, Chapter 2.3.

12 John Collins *Are All Christians Ministers?*, Brunswick Victoria, Australia: E. J. Dwyer , 1992.

13 Romans 11.13, 12.7, 15.31.

14 Romans 15.25

15 See Chapter Four p. 43 for a discussion of this.

16 Elisabeth Schüssler Fiorenza 'Missionaries, Apostles, Co-workers' in *Feminist Theology A Reader*, (ed.) Ann Loades London: SPCK, 1990, pp. 60-5.

17 1 Thessalonians 3:2, Ambrosiaster Pelagius, Basil Theodore and others have diakonos, Nestle/Aland has sunergon

18 Phil 1.1 and 1 Tim 3.8. John Ziesler, *Pauline Christianity*. Oxford: Oxford University Press, Revised Edition 1990), p. 137 says: 'Although we are uncertain about the exact nature of these offices, the letters' recipients clearly were not, and their knowledge can be taken for granted.

19 1 Corinthians 3.5, 6, 6.4, 2 Corinthians11.15 (twice), 11.23.

201 Raymond E. Brown, Joseph Fitzmyer, Roland E. Murphy, (eds.), *New Jerome Biblical Commentary,* London: Geoffrey Chapman, 1990.

21 1 Corinthians 12.5, 16.15 and 2 Corinthians 3.7, 8, 9, 4.1, 5.18, 6.3, 8.4, 9.1,12, 13 and 11.8.

22 *New Jerome Biblical Commentary*, p814.

23 1Tim. 3.8

24 1Tim 3.8 and 1Tim 3.12

25 See *The New Greek Testament* Stuttgart: Deutsche Bibelgesellschaft,

1993, pp. 700–1 for manuscripts offering this version.

26 1 Thessalonians 3.2

27 Acts 14.23

28 Raymond E. Brown, *The Churches the Apostles Left Behind*. London,

Geoffrey Chapman, 1984), pp. 32–3.

29 C. E. B. Cranfield, 'Diakonia in the New Testament' in *Service in Christ*, (ed.) James
  I. McCord and T. H. L. Parker, p. 37.

30 Howard Marshall says 'Luke describes the effect of the new appointment in terms of
  an increase in Christian Witness'. *The Acts of the Apostles* Leicester, England: Inter-
  Varsity Press, 1980, p. 127.

31 Heb. 6.10, 1 Peter 1.12 and 1Peter 4.10.

Chapter Six

1 James Monroe Barnett *The Diaconate* Valley Forge, PA., Trinity Press
International, revised edition, 1995, p. 43

2 The Council of Nicaea (325 AD) in canon 18 reduced and restricted the work of the
  order of deacons. www.nwt.org/d-chronology.htm

3 See Barnett *The Diaconate* p. 102 quoting Jerome the presbyter.

4 *New Jerome Biblical Commentary*, p. 1345.

5 *A New Eusebius*, (ed.) J. Stevenson (London, SPCK, 1995), p. 8.

6 *The Epistle of St. Ignatius of Antioch to the Magnesians*, translated by Charles H.
  Hoole, (ed.) By Friar Martin Fonyonet Gonzalez for the St. Pachomius Library
  Chapter   2.1   Internet   Address
  www.ocf.org/OrthodoxPage/reading/St.Pachomius/Greek/ignatius.magnesians.html
  1984

7 Barnett, *The Diaconate*, p. 48.

8 Jill Pinnock *The Deacon's Ministry* p. 11

9 Torrance in 'The Eldership in the Reformed Church' refers to Jewish law which entitled a community of one hundred and twenty strong being allowed its own sanhedrin numbering seven appointed by the laying on of hands. Calvin in Institutes of the Christian Religion accuses deacons of the Church of Rome of claiming descent from Levites. The Levites were consecrated and set apart to serve the tabernacle in every way but that of the priest. There are some parallels.

10 *A New Eusebius*, p. 172

11 *The Epistle of St Ignatius to the Magnesians* Chapter 6.1

12 Justin Martyr 'Apology 1. 61-7' *A New Eusebius*, pp. 63-64, also quoted in

Hall *The Deacon's Ministry*, p. 13.

13 Ambrosiaster, 101.5, *in 'Pseudo-Augustine, Quaestions Veteris et Novi Testamen CXXVII*, trans Souter in *Corpus Scriptorum Ecclesiasticorum 50*, 196. Quoted in Barnett, *The Diaconate*, p.103.

14 *Bishop, Priest, Deacon* (www.catholic.com/answers/tracts/_3orders.htm, May 1996)

15 Charitable is used throughout this work in the sense as defined *in A New Dictionary of Christian Ethics* (ed.) John Macquarrie and James Childress (London: SCM, 1986}, p 84. 'The term charity is used especially in Roman Catholic theology to refer to the love of God and neighbour mandated by Jesus in his summary of the law and evoked by God's love; charity is also one of the three infused theological virtues.'

16 Jill Pinnock, 'History of the Diaconate' *The Deacon's Ministry*

17 The Congregation for the Clergy and the Congregation for Catholic Education, *The Permanent Diaconate* London: Catholic Truth Society 1998, p. 14.

18 John St.H. Gibaut. 'Sequential and Direct Ordination' in *Anglican Orders and Ordinations: Essays and Reports from the Interim Conference at Jarvenpää, Finland at the International Anglican Liturgical Consultation,* (ed.) David R. Holeton Cambridge: Grove Books, 1997, p. 36.

19 The grading of orders.

20 Barnett *The Diaconate*, p. 105.

21 For example Ignatius of Antioch, Hippolytus, Jerome the Presbyter and

others

22 Ignatius of Antioch, *Epistle to the Magnesians*.

23 Barnett, *The Diaconate*, p. 102

24 Eusebius represented Dionysius, bishop of Alexandria, at the Council of Antioch in 264. Athanasius played a leading part in the Council of Nicaea in 325 while still a deacon and before succeeding Alexander as bishop.

25 John StH. Gibaut 'Sequential and Direct Ordination', *in Anglican Orders and Ordinations*, p. 36

26 Gibaut p. 40.

27 Gibaut., p. 40.

28 Kevin Flynn, 'Once a Deacon' in *Anglican Orders and Ordinations* .

29 'The history of the Diaconate' *The Deacon's Ministry*, ed. Christine Hall

(Leominster: Gracewing, 1992), p 20.

30 Barnett, *The Diaconate*, p. 84.

31 Barnett, *The Diaconate*, p. 84..

32 Barnett, *The Diaconate*, p. 85.

33 Understandings of ordination are discussed in Chapter Nine.

34 I have been present at a cathedral in France at Auray, when for the great festival of Our Lady, several Archbishops and perhaps a dozen bishops grace the cathedral. In a vast outdoor mass, the presidency is taken by the archbishops and the bishops take the deacon's role in distributing the communion to the people in the crowds.

35 see *Bishop, Priest and Deacon in the Church of Sweden*, a letter from the bishops concerning the ministry of the Church, The Bishop's Conference, 1990

36 Barnett, *The Diaconate*, pp. 67-68

37 Barnett, *The Diaconate*, pp. 67-68.

38 G. Barrois, 'On Mediaeval Charities' in (ed.), McCord, James I. and Parker, T. H. L., *Service in Christ*.

39 J. K. S. Reid, 'Diakonia in the Thought of Calvin' in (ed.), McCord, James I. and Parker, T. H. L., in *Service in Christ* p. 107.

40 It would seem to be the transitional deacon for whom Luther had this dislike.

41 James Atkinson 'Diakonia at the time of the Reformation' in in (ed.), McCord, James I. and Parker, T. H. L., *Service in Christ*, p. 82.

42 Luther 'De captivate Babylonica 1520, WA.6.566.34-567.5 quoted by James,Atkinson 'Diakonia at the time of the Reformation' in (ed.), McCord, James I. and Parker, T. H. L., *Service in Christ* p. 83

43 James Atkinson, 'Diakonia at the time of the Reformation' in (ed.), McCord, James I. and Parker, T. H. L., *Service in Christ*, p. 81.

44 JamesAtkinson, 'Diakonia at the time of the Reformation' in (ed.), McCord, James I. and Parker, T. H. L., Service in Christ p. 84.

45 For a more modern exposition of the reformers' thesis see Karl Barth, 'The Ministry of the Community', Church Dogmatics, Vol. IV, Part 3.

46 James Atkinson, 'Diakonia at the time of the Reformation' in (ed.), McCord, James I. and Parker, T. H. L., *Service in Christ*, p. 82.

47 Calvin suggests also that the diaconate has two functions, the first of which is administration and the second distribution of charity. See *The Methodist Diaconal Order, A Report for Conference 1993*. London: Methodist Church, 1992, para 5.3.

48 See Barnett, *The diaconate*, p 104 for a description of cursus honorum and the development of the 'vertical' structures to replace the 'horizontal organic'.

49 Jill Pinnock, 'The History of the Diaconate' in *The Deacon's Minist*ry, p. 20.

50 Gibaut, 'Sequential and Direct Ordination', p. 36.

51 Alistair E. McGrath,. *A Life of John Calvin*. Basil Blackwell, 1990, p. 80.

52 John Calvin, *Institutes of the Christian Religion*, translated by Henry Beveridge London: James Clarke, 1956 Vol 4 Part 4 Chapter 3. See also (de captivitate Babylonica 1520 quoted by James Atkinson 'Diakonia at the time of the Reformation' in (ed.), McCord, James I. and Parker, T. H. L., *Service in Christ*, p. 83.

Chapter Seven

1 *Diakonhjemmet Hospital and College, a brief history* (Internet http://www.diakonhjemmet.no/dnd/eng-dnd.htm. 1998.)

2 John Padberg 'Understanding a Tradition of Religious Life' in *Religious Life* (ed Gerald A. Arbuckle and David L. Fleming Slough: St Paul Publications, 1990, p. 14

3 The Bruderhaus was patterned on a religious community without vows or church magisterium usually associated with formal 'orders'.

4 Jill Pinnock, 'The History of the Diaconate', in *The Deacon's Ministry*, p. 22

5   The Moravian Church is a small denomination very active in the mission field. Refounded under the guidance of Count Zinzendorf in 1772 it claims descent from the Hussites and the United Brethren church founded in Bohemia by Peter Chelcic in 1467.

6   Florence Nightingale came there in 1850 to train as a nurse.

7   The 'motherhouse' is the base for a dispersed religious order. The term is also used of the training centre or home from which religious operate into the community.

8 'Bishop Priest and Deacon in the church of Sweden' A letter from the bishops concerning the ministry of the Church, the Bishop's Conference, 1990. Internet address http://www.svkyran.se/arkeb/biskmote/beng901/amb3eng3.htm

9   'Bishop Priest and Deacon in the church of Sweden'

10   The last NCH Sister retired in 1997.

11 Kenneth B. Garlick 'Centenary Roots of Diaconal *Order' Methodist Recorder* London, August 2, 1990, p. 14

12 The curriculum included training in Mission work: (a) in connection with circuits, or congregations. (b) In connection with Mission Centres. (In villages, or groups of villages). (d) In Foreign Missions.

13 Constance M. Oosthuizen, *Conquerors through Christ, The Deaconess Order of South Africa* Port Shepstone, 1990, p. 2.

14 The 'Biblewomen' were local Tamil and Singhalese women trained in basic evangelism and with some training in hygiene and first aid. These women could go and work amongst the village women at times when the deaconesses would not be acceptable.

15 'Letter to Mr Maltby' from A. Lockwood, Chairman of women's work, Kalmunai, Ceylon, 1918.

16 'It is of importance that they (the deaconesses) should be trained to do the utmost that is possible at the smallest imaginable cost.' R.T.R. writing in the Methodist Recorder of March 25, 1897.

17 NIV

18 Barnett, *The Diaconate a Full and Equal Order*, p. 217

19 John Collins, *Are All Christians Ministers*, pp. 157-8.

20 One of the strategies suggested as part of the project was to have an article on the subject published in the *Epworth Review*. A discussion of Collins' view of Ministry and the Word was published in the October 2000 issue.

21 The Roman Catholic General Norms For Restoring The Permanent Diaconate in the Latin Church, the decisions of the United Methodist Conference of 1996 in restoring a Permanent Diaconate and the Anglican Lutheran document The Diaconate as Ecumenical opportunity are all pointing to a changed view of diaconal ministry.

22 Secretariat for the Diaconate, National conference of Bishops/United States Catholic Conference. *Worldwide statistics on the Diaconate as of January 1996.*

23 *The Permanent Diaconate* London: Catholic Truth Society, 1998, p. 104.

24 Rev. David Forsyth, Dunkeld News, 26th October, 1997. A quarterly journal under the patronage of Bishop Vincent Logan, Bishop of Dunkeld

25 Papal address on permanent deacons to the plenary session of the Congregation for Clergy, 30 November, 1997 (text from L'Osservatore Romano)

26 PRE September 1997 - Hallam Diocesan Magazine

27 Http:/members.laol.net/gkcarr/Who_deacons.htm, the personal web page of Deacon George Carr of the Diocese of Lake Charles.

28 In the United States Priestly ordinations have fallen from 994 in 1965 to 509 in 1998 and the numbers of religious brothers and sisters have been reduced by 50% over the same period. In formation from the National Conference of Catholic Bishops home page, www.nccbuscc.org/vocations/statistics.htm.

29 This word is attributed to Karl Rahner by Edward Echlin in *The Deacon's Ministry.*

30 Dr Christina Baxter, Chairman of the house of Laity quoted by Barry Rogerson 'The diaconate: Taking the ecumenical opportunity?' *Community - Unity - Communion* (ed.) Colin Podmore, London: Church House Publishing, 1998. p 204

31 General Synod of the Church of England, *Deacons in the Ministry of the Church* , London: Church House Publishing, 1988, p. 66.

32 *The Diaconate as Ecumenical Opportunity* , The Hanover Report of the Anglican-Lutheran International Commission , London: Anglican Communion Publications, 1996, p. 22.

33 General Synod of the church of England, *Deacons in the Ministry of the Church* , p. 98.

34 Barnett *The Diaconate*, p. 175.

35 In 1993 the Bishops of Chelmsford and St Albans suggested to their diocesan Synods that progress on this matter was urgent and in 1998 the Bishop of Ely brought a Diocesan Synod motion to General Synod asking for an inquiry into the renewed diaconate.

36 *Bishop, Priest and Deacon in the Church of Sweden,* http:/www.svkyrkan.se/arkeb/biskmote/beng901/amb3eng3.htm

37 Anglican Consultative Council and The Lutheran World Federation *The Diaconate as Ecumenical Opportunity*.

38 Report of the Lutheran-Episcopal Drafting Team, (Chicago, Evangelical Lutheran Church in America, 1998), Paragraph 9.

39 Graham Cook and Bob Day*, Church Related Community Work in the United Reform Church* URC Mission Council, 1998), p. 9.

40 Jean Robinson in *A hundred years on and . . .A Renewed Order*, Birmingham, Methodist Diaconal Order, 1990, p. 5.

41 In 1999 the Methodist Church introduced a new process which involves a period of training before offering for ministry, with the intent that this should allow for an opportunity vocational discernment.

42 ‹Community in modern sociology is used in a general and deliberately vague way.' This definition, as supplied in *A Dictionary of Socio*logy, (ed) G. Duncan Mitchell, London: Routledge and Kegan Paul, 1968, p32, would equally apply to its use within the Methodist Church. It would generally seem to be used to refer to work of a sociological, rather than spiritual nature undertaken in the local community to which the particular congregation or circuit would claim to be related to.

43 The Constitutional Practice and Discipline of the Methodist Church.

44 Methodist ministers and deacons are 'received into full connexion' by the Conference before they are ordained. The term implies a recognition of their ministry by the whole Methodist Church.

45 As a dispersed community deacons meet 'in convocation' each year to affirm their membership of the Order, to conduct business and to share in fellowship.

46 Anthony Bash 'Deacons and Diaconal Ministry' in *Theology*, January/February 1999, p 37.

47 Used in the sense of 'to exhibit the image of'.

48 T. F. Torrance, 'Service in Jesus Christ' in Service in Christ, p. 13.

49 The baptism of adults in the early church was by full immersion and it was the duty of deaconesses to assist at the baptism, taking the female candidates into the water and robing them afterwards.

50 Pope John Paul II. ‹Papal Address on Permanent Deacons›. (Internet Address http//:www.tasc.ac.uk/cc/briefing/9601/9601004.htm, 17th April, 1998)

51 Trevor Rowe, 'The Reformation of the Diaconal Order', *Epworth Review* , Vol 24 (Peterborough: Methodist Publishing House, 1997), p. 63. (My italics)

52 Gordon Wakefield, 'Diakonia in the Methodist Church Today' in McCord, James I. and Parker, T. H. L., (ed.), *Service in Christ,*

53 Wakefield, Service in Christ, p. 185.

54 The Methodist Communion Stewards were for many years called 'poor stewards' as it was part of their role to take up a collection for the poor at the communion service.

55 Wakefield, *Service in Christ*, p. 187. (My italics).

56 See definitions on p. 107 but it needs to be understood that the terms 'minister' and 'ministry' can only be applied to presbyters under present rules.

Chapter Eight

1   The Methodist Church at national level is referred to as the Connexion.

2   See Chapter Three, pp. 55-56

3   Authority to preside at Holy Communion is not given to deacons in the Methodist Church by their ordination. This parallels the practice in all other churches and in the

tradition. Within the Methodist tradition and Church Order, Conference can grant an authorisation, where there is deprivation, for others to preside within the area of deprivation only.

4   The preaching appointments in a Methodist circuit are arranged by the superintendent minister and are presented on a document traditionally called 'The Plan'.

5   See page

6   Gordon Wakefield, *Service in Christ*, p. 186, quotes Alfred Barrett: 'The diaconate is a plastic office, which may be moulded by circumstances and necessity.'

7 This is not personal to the particular holder of the role. The previous incumbent engendered a very similar feeling and there was much pain when the church rejected her application to become a presbyter

Chapter Nine

1   William W. Emilsen, "The Face of Christ" *Theology*, Vol. 110, No. 7.

2   The Congregation for the Clergy and The Congregation for Catholic Education, *The Permanent Diaconate*, p. 104.

3   There are Lutheran churches which ordain, and churches with their roots in the Episcopal tradition which prefer consecration.

4   Anglican Consultative Council and the Lutheran World Federation *The Diaconate as Ecumenical Opportunity* London: Anglican Communion Publications, 1996, p. 23. The Congregation for the Clergy and The Congregation for Catholic Education, The Permanent Diaconate (London: Catholic Truth Society, 1998), p. 75.

5   Bishop, Priest and Deacon in the Church of Sweden, http://www.svkyran.se/arkeb/biskmote/beng901/

amb3emg3.htm.

6   Anglican Consultative Council and the Lutheran World Federation *The Diaconate as Ecumenical Opportunity*, p. 23.

7   See page 91.

8   Anglican Consultative Council and the Lutheran World Federation *The Diaconate as Ecumenical Opportunity*, p. 22.

9   The Congregation for the Clergy and the Congregation for Catholic Education The Permanent Diaconate, pp. 88-108 and 112-14.

10 Frederick Herzog. "Diakonia in Modern Times, Eighteenth-Twentieth Centuries" in Service in Christ, p148.

11 United Reformed Church, *Commission on the Ministry, Report to the General Assembly*, 1975, p. 6.

12 See Chapter Seven, page 93.

13 The starting point for describing the deacon's ministry is often "Deacons don't . . ." this will include the obvious deacons don't preside at holy communion but regularly will include deacon's don't conduct baptisms, funerals, weddings or have pastoral care. See Chapter 7 p. 95.

14 The Congregation for the Clergy and The Congregation for Catholic Education, *The Permanent Diaconate* p. 97.

15 Donald Coggan, *The Servant-Son* London: Triangle, 1995, . p 88.

16 Here "representative" takes on several of its meanings - representative person, example, someone who makes representation to another on our behalf. For Christians Christ is the ideal image.

17 Alan Richardson, *A Dictionary of Christian Theology* London: SCM, 1969, p. 289.

18 The Methodist Church. Methodist Conference 1996, Agenda, Peterborough: Methodist Publishing House, p. 816, para 3.3.

19 Matthew 6.1

20 Matthew 5.16

21 Nicholas Lash. *Service of Homecoming*, a paper given at The Second National Diaconate Assembly of England and Wales, May 1998.

22   Jim Liggett, *Some Reflections on Diaconate* (www.nwt.org/d-theology.htm, 1996), p. 1. Father Liggett is an Anglican priest in the Diocese of North West Texas and his comments concern his denomination's discussions on the permanent diaconate.

23 Anglican Consultative Council and the Lutheran World Federation *The Diaconate as Ecumenical Opportunity*, p. 26.

24 Conversation at local preachers training day.

25 See page 113.

26 See page 114.

Select Bibliography

Aitchison, Ronald, *Wesley Deaconess Order, Methodist Diaconal Order*, Newtown: Modik, 1994.

_____ 'The Lost Deacon', *Epworth Review,* Vol 27 (October 2000). Peterborough: Methodist Publishing House, 2000.

Anglican Consultative Council and The Lutheran World Federation*, The Diaconate as Ecumenical Opportunity,* London: Anglican Communion Publications, 1996

Barnett, James Monroe*, The Diaconate,*Valley Forge, P.A.: Trinity Press International, Revised Edition,1995.

Bartlett, David L, *Ministry in the New Testament*, Minneapolis: Fortress Press, 1993.

Bash, Anthony, 'Deacons and Diaconal Ministry', *Theology,* London: SPCK, January/February 1999.

Beasley, John D, *The Bitter Cry Heard and Heeded,* London: South London Mission, 1990.

Bowie, Fiona, *Beguine Spirituality,* London: SPCK, 1989.

Bradfield, William, *The Life of the Reverend Thomas Bowman Stephenson,* London: Charles Kelly, 1913.

Collins, John N *Diakonia: Re-interpreting the Ancient Sources*, New York & Oxford: Oxford University Press, 1990.

_____. *Are All Christians Ministers*, Newtown, Australia: E. J. Dwyer,   1992

Congregation for Catholic Education and Congregation for the Clergy*, The Permanent Diaconate,* London: Catholic Truth Society, 1998.

Flynn, Kevin. 'Once a Deacon'. in by David R. Holeton, (ed), *Anglican Orders and Ordinations: Essays and Reports from the Interim Conference at Jarvenpää, Finland*

at the International Anglican Liturgical Consultation,
Cambridge: Grove Books, 1997

General Synod of the Church of England, *Deacons in the Ministry of the Church, A Report to the House of Bishops,*
London: Church House Publishing, 1988.

Gibaut, John St. H, 'Sequential and Direct Ordination', in
by David R. Holeton, (ed), *Anglican Orders and Ordinations: Essays and Reports from the Interim Conference at Jarvenpää, Finland at the International Anglican Liturgical Consultation,* Cambridge: Grove Books, 1997

Hall, Christine and Hannaford, Robert, (eds.),*Order and Ministry*, Leominster: Gracewing Fowler Wright Books, 1996.

Hall, Christine, (ed.), *The Deacon's Ministry,* Leominster: Gracewing Fowler Wright Books, 1991.

McCord, James I. and Parker, T. H. L., (ed.), *Service In Christ: Essays Presented to Karl Barth on his 80th Birthday,* London: Epworth Press, 1966

Mar Gregorious, Paulos, *The Meaning and Nature of Diakonia,* Geneva: WCC Publications, 1988.

Methodist Church, *The Methodist Diaconal Order, Report to Conference 1993,* Peterborough: Methodist Publishing House, 1993.

_____. *The Minutes of Conference, 1916.,* Peterborough: Methodist Publishing House, 1916.

_____, *The Ministry of the People of God, Report to Conference 1988.,* Peterborough: Methodist Publishing House, 1988.

Methodist Council, *1997 Diaconate Report - Fourth Draft, Peterborough,* Methodist Publishing House, 1997.

Methodist Diaconal Order, *The Windsor Statement on the Diaconate,* St George's House Windsor, 1997.

Mullan, David S., *Diakonia and the Moa,* Auckland, New Zealand: Methodist Theological College, 1984.

Nowell, Robert, *The Ministry of Service*, London: Burns & Oates, 1968.

Olson, Jeanine E, *One Ministry, Many Roles*, St. Louis, USA: Concordia Publishing House, 1992.

Oosthuizen, Constance M, *Conquerors Through Christ, The Deaconess Order of South Africa*, Port Shepstone, 1990.

Plater, Ormonde, *Many Servants*, Boston, Massachusetts: Cowley Publications, 1991.

Rogerson, Barry, 'The Diaconate: Taking the ecumenical opportunity?', in Colin Podmore, *Community - Unity - Communion: Essays in Honour of Mary Tanner*, London: Church House Publishing, 1998.

Rose, Doris M. Baptist Deaconesses, London: Carey Kingsgate Press, 1954.

Rowe, Trevor. "The Re-formation of the Diaconal Order", *Epworth Review* Vol 24 (April 1997). Peterborough: Methodist Publishing House, 1997..

Schweizer, Eduard. *Church Order in the New Testament*, Translated by Frank Clarke. London: SCM Press, 1961.

Stephenson, T. Bowman. *Concerning Sisterhoods*, London: C. H. Kelly, 1890.

Swensson, Gerd, ed. *The Churches and the Diaconate*, Translated David Thompson, Uppsala: Bokförlaget Pro Veritate, 1985.

USEFUL INTERNET SITES

Diakonhjemmet Hospital and College. Internet address http://www.diakonhjemmet.no/english/index.htm.

Deacons in the Uniting Church in Australia. Internet address http://www.client.ucaqld.com.au/~jjohn/deacweb/uca/about.htm

http://www.stephenministries.com/

Diaconal Ministry in the United Church of Canada Internet
address http://www.uccan.org/mpe/diaconal.htm
United Methodist Church:
http://www.umc.org/churchleadership/ordainedministry/dea
cons/
Catholic deacons: http://www.deaconsplace.org
Dace: http://societies.anglican.org/dace/intro.htm
Diakonia: http://www.drae.org/

ABOUT THE AUTHOR

Ronnie Aitchison Trained for the Diaconate at Queens College and went into his first appointment in Castleford in 1994. He was invited to study for a Master of Ministry and Theology at UTU, Sheffield in 1996. The original book was the product of that thesis. During his time in Skelmersdale he researched for a PhD with Potchefstroomse University on the history and Theology of the Wesley Deaconesses Overseas Missions and was awarded that in 2004. He left Skelmersdale in 2005 and spent three Years as Synod Secretary for Liverpool District. He is at present a Supernumerary Deacon in the Aire and Calder Circuit.

―――――――――――――

Printed in Great Britain
by Amazon

32713648R00126